CONTENTS

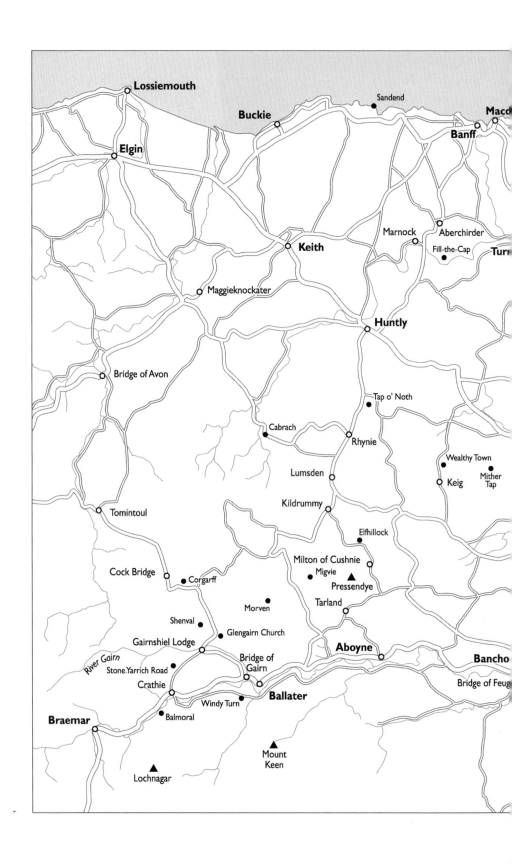

The Road to Maggieknockater

Exploring Aberdeen and the North-east through its Place names

Robert Smith

Birlinn

First published in 2004 by
Birlinn Limited
West Newington House
10 Newington Road
Edinburgh EH9 1QS

www.birlinn.co.uk

ISBN 1 84158 321 9

British Library Cataloguing-in-Publication Data
A catalogue record for this book is available from the British Library

Typeset by Textype, Cambridge
Printed and bound by GraphyCems, Spain

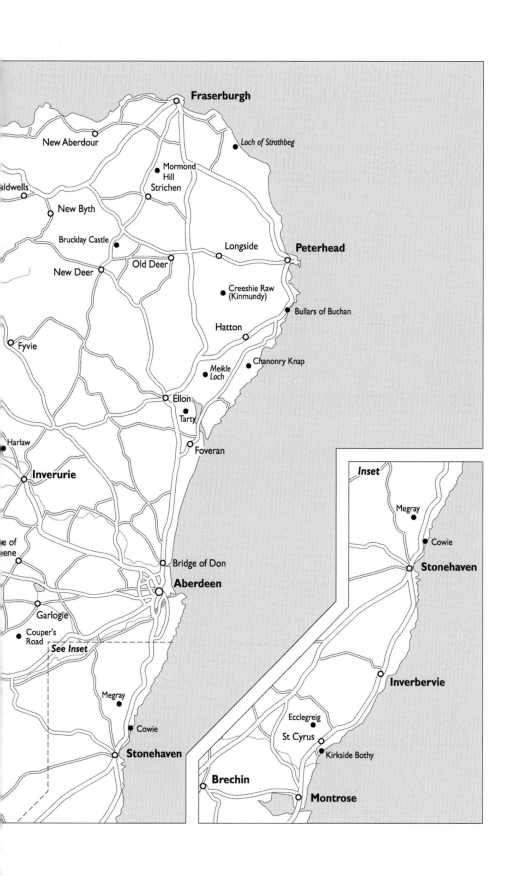

1
MAGGIEKNOCKATER

It all began on the road to Maggieknockater. Many years ago, I saw a newspaper advertisement offering a farmhouse holiday on Speyside. It sounded a good idea at the time, so I made my booking and in due course piled my wife and two youngsters into my old banger and headed north.

It was the name that attracted me. Maggieknockater turned out to be a tiny hamlet near Craigellachie. It was the sort of place you could pass

The road to Maggieknockater – 'the sort of place you could pass through without noticing it.'

through without noticing it was there. Still, the countryside around it was spectacular and we were lucky enough to have a car. We could explore the wonders of Speyside. Next day the car broke down and the local garage had to send away for a spare part. It would have to be Shanks' mare.

Another family joined us at the farm. We sat on a high bank at the roadside and watched them arrive in a taxi, dressed in their Sunday best, ill-attired for life on a farm, and we thought, 'hmm! how will they cope with all this?' They were from Aberdeen, a banker and his wife and two kids, and we got on famously.

We were cut off from the outside world. Nobody ever came to Maggieknockater and little traffic passed through it. The highlight of our holiday came when we waylaid an ice-cream van passing through the village and stood guzzling ice-cream cones on the main road.

There were no luxuries at the Maggieknockater farm. Plain fare and no frills was the order of the day. For dinner, we ate pigeons shot by the farmer, surreptitiously spitting out the pellets that went free with the meal. Live music was provided in the evening by the farmer, who was as nimble with a melodeon as he was with a gun.

Looking back, I can't remember any of us having any regrets. Package holidays, coach tours, trips abroad – nothing measured up to that week at Maggieknockater. I never solved the mystery of the name when I was there. It was a long time before I did and by then I was totally wrapped up in the subject of place names: their origin, their history, their folklore.

Maggieknockater wasn't always the dead-and-alive place it is now. Up until some fifty years ago it had a mission hall, which was converted into a private house. It also had a school, which was closed down and razed to the ground, and it had an emporium and a post office. All gone.

It even had a castle, Gauldwell Castle, which must have given Maggieknockater a certain historical dignity. It was formerly known as the castle of Bucharin (Boharm) and was in the possession of the family of De Moravia of Duffus. Its chapel is mentioned as early as 1203. But they knocked the castle down, too, and now all that is left of it is a rickle of stones among the trees at Gauldwell Farm

The link with Boharm is intriguing, for in the kirk session records of the parish of Boharm in 1677 the name Marg McKnuketer appears. But there is nothing to show that she was the Maggie who gave her name to the hamlet on the road to Craigellachie.

Correspondence about the name started up in *Scottish Notes and Queries* in 1924. One writer thought that Maggie Knockater was probably a corruption of the name Mac-in ucater. He recalled seeing it in the Privy Council Register and said that the name meant 'son of the fuller (cloth worker)'.

The most intriguing explanation came from a retired schoolmaster, who said he had seen the seventeenth-century session records of Boharm and had found several references to a Maggie Macknockater. This Maggie appeared from time to time before the session for offences such as 'unseemly conduct, bawling on the Lord's day and so on'.

The schoomaster concluded that she had lived in or about the place that bore her name. This was at the junction of the roads leading to Glenrinnes and Glenlivet and would probably have been a resting place for drovers with their cattle and for smugglers passing from the glens with their whisky in casks slung over their ponies.

'If this supposition is correct,' wrote the schoolmaster, 'these worthies would speak of one of the houses (which presumably Maggie occupied as a shebeen) as Maggie Knockater's. Shebeens of this kind were common all over the north at the beginning of the century, generally situated near commons and at cross-roads, and near cattle market stances, and they were often familiarly known by the names of the good ladies who kept them.'

So there it is – there really was a Maggie who once lived in that peaceful, god-forsaken place called Maggieknockater. I think, sometime, I will wander down to the Glenrinnes crossroads to see if there is still a shebeen there, where I can raise a glass to the woman who first kindled my interest in place names.

The study of place names is known officially as onomastics, a dreary name for such a fascinating subject. While serious students of onomastics search diligently for the orgins of names, I look for the untold stories behind them. Place names can tell you many things. They can tell you about the countryside, the weather, about elfs and fairies (see Chapter 3), about the hills and burns, about myths and legends, about forgotten settlements, about the raiding cateran, about ruined crofts and farms, and about the folk who once lived in them.

There are signposts that lead you into this magical world – signposts at farms or at the end of farm tracks: Cauldwells, or Caul'walls, as we called it, where I hyowed neeps for an uncle when I was a loon; Wuddy Hill at Old Deer in Buchan, a name that came from *widdie*, 'a gallows'; Pyke's Cairn in the Cabach, where a farmer perished in the snow in 1777; Seggat, where Lewis Grassic Gibbon was born; Quartalehouse at Stuartfield, which had nothing to do with a drinking howff, but came from the Gaelic *Gort-kie-mor*, meaning 'a field between two streams'.

When I was driving through Buchan on one occasion I saw a signpost near Strichen which said Fridayhill. I jammed on the brakes, did a quick reverse, and shot up Fridayhill. I wanted to know if there was a Saturdayhill and a Sundayhill and so on. The farmer told me that it used to be called FREEday hill, so it's anybody's guess what that meant. I did see a reference later to FREDDAYhill, and that apparently did mean Friday.

I was also told that the neighbouring farm, Grassiehill, used to be called Gressiehill, and I found out that this came from a Gaelic word, *Greasaich*, meaning 'a shoemaker' – a souter. So here again names uncovered just a little bit of the past.

The Rev. James Brown Johnston, Falkirk, author of *Place Names of Scotland* (1892), had this to say about the place-name game:

> Every place-name means something, or at least once meant
> something. Only in the degenerate nineteenth century had
> men begun to coin silly, meaningless names. Only within
> late years could a Dickens or a Thackeray have had the
> chance of satirising his neighbour for calling No.153 in a
> dinghy back street, full 20 feet above the level of the sea,
> *Mount Pleasant*, or for christening an ugly brick house, in
> full sight of a gasworks, *Belle Vue*.

Early place-name books, packing in the entries, had little space to spare for background material. Maggieknockater turned up in *Place Names of Scotland*, but there was no sugggestion of possible alternatives – no hint that Maggie might have been a real, live person. It simply said that the name came from *mag an fhucaadair*, 'field of the fuller'.

James Johnston is said to have been a pioneer in the study and elucidation of place names, but it has also been said that he was 'seriously off the mark when dealing with etymologies'. In the preface to the third reprint of his book in 1934, he says that Professor W.J. Watson's *Celtic Place-Names of Scotland*, 1926, was by far the most important work on the subject, but he also criticises some of the professor's 'serious omissions', including such landmarks as 'a great ben like Wyvis' and 'a great river like the Tweed'. He goes on, 'and if a visitor goes to Deeside, he will find no help about Aboyne or Invercauld or even about Balmoral and great Lochnagar.'

He also mentions a number of people who had been 'of very real service' to him. Among them was James Macdonald, whose *Place Names in Strathbogie* was published in 1891. Macdonald thought that the subject of place-names had received serious attention in only a few districts in Scotland. There would have to be a lot of research by individual students before it would be possible to undertake a comprehensive work on the place names of Scotland with any hope of success.

Eight years later, Macdonald started to pave the way with *Place Names of West Aberdeenshire*, but died while half-way through it. His nephew, C.E. Troup, organised its completion, with help from well-known experts. Half a century later, William M. Alexander wrote a revised edition of Macdonald's work, using, among other things, notes from Francis C. Diack's *Inscriptions of Pictland*.

In 1984, Adam Watson and Elizabeth Allan crowned a decade of spare-time place-name study with *Place Names of Upper Deeside*. The book was based largely on information from 260 local people and included nearly 7,000 place-names. 'We halted the collection,' they wrote, 'when we had asked for the names of every field, ruin, hill, corrie, stream, and wood, and when over half the new informants were producing no further names for our list.' It was a superb publication, all the more so because they had no experience of place name study until 1973, when the research was started by Adam, initially with the help of John Duff, Braemar, joined later by Betty Allan.

Included in the acknowledgements were the names of Professor W.F.H. Nicolaisen, then head of the Scottish Place-Name Survey, and Ian Fraser, who was appointed research assistant to the survey in 1965, and later editor. It was around that time that I began to be interested in place names. In 1984 I went to Edinburgh to see Ian about a series of place-name articles I was doing for the *Aberdeen Press and Journal*. The series was based on the tales that arose from the names, as it is in this book, not overwhelmed by linguistic analysis or toponymics – another word likely to scare-off non-professionals.

Bill Nicolaisen, who, like myself, has written for *Leopard* Magazine, once drew attention to what had been said by that noted folklorist, the Rev. Walter Gregor, in a report he presented to the New Spalding Club in 1887. Gregor dealt with the connection between topography and folklore and two lines of his report echo my own thinking. 'The main object of topography,' he wrote, 'is a collection of the names of all places (in the North-east). Connected with many of these are legends and rhymes which should be carefully chronicled.'

Ian Fraser's paper about the Scottish Place Name Survey, which was founded by Edinburgh University in 1950, points out that until then the field of onomastics had been carried on mainly by private individuals. Although this had resulted in several notable collections of place-name studies, mostly on a county basis, there was still a real need for research to be conducted on a nationwide scale.

He recounts how the survey had to take 'unusual measures' to collect rapidly disappearing material. In 1974 he was approached by the Scottish Women's Rural Institute, who had arranged a local history and place-names competition among their branches. Over 200 six-inch maps were distributed to individuals and branches of the institute, involving the surveying of some 350 farms throughout Scotland. Over the next few years, collections of field-names were built up, some extremely detailed.

So much has changed since that happened. New technology has arrived, interest has grown, and a Scottish place name database has been set up. A news sheet on the database, put out on the Internet, showed that it contained approximately 8,000 place names, with about 13,500 historical forms. These included all the place names within the pre-1975 county of Banff, and the parishes of Old and New Deer, which together contained 450 place-names.

'The first decade of the survey,' wrote Ian Fraser, 'concentrated on building up an archive on place-name forms of paper slips, with many thousands of hours being spent transferring, by hand, in ink, the documentary forms from such important Scottish records as the Register of the Great Seal, the Retours, the Origins Parochiales, and many others.

'Today, with sophisticated electronic means at our fingertips, we take the labours of half a century ago very much for granted. We now deal with data so rapidly that the workers and researchers of 1951 would have regarded such processes as science fiction.'

Whatever the new technology, volunteer collectors can still play a vital role in the name game. I was given an illustration of this recently when I went to the Durris area of Kincardine to look for names and found I was walking in the footsteps of an earlier collector. I had been drawn to Durris by a place-name rhyme I had seen, which went:

Calladrum an' Balladrum,
An' Mains o' Blairydryne,
Quithelhead an' Newton
An' Muckle Barns syne.

Later, I saw a report from the Scottish Place-Name Survey in which a Banchory woman, Moira Forsyth, told what happened when she offered to collect names in Durris parish. She was given field collection sheets and maps and set off on her great adventure. She spoke to eleven farmers and collected the field-names of fourteen farms. Whether or not she saw the Muckle Barns or any of the other farms in the rhyme I never discovered, but she was given a courteous welcome, 'after some initial bemusement at the interest in the names of their "parks" '.

2

A MAGIC CARPET

A magic carpet that will sweep you away to strange and wonderful places – that's the place-name game. It will take you to Pennystone Green in Logie Coldstone, where the drovers rested their cattle on their way south, or to the Wormie Hillock at Rhynie, where you can see the grave-mound of a dragon, or it will take you to the Kinker Stone above the farm of Fernybrae at the Chapel of Garioch, where a rock with a cavity contains water which is said to cure your kink-hoast (whooping cough).

It may also carry you to Bleezes at Oyne, a local name for Old Westhall, which is on a hill about half a mile west of the parish church. There was a public house there at one time, but whether or not the customers were always 'bleezing' is not recorded.

Alternatively, you can fly away on the magic carpet to Egypt. When I was searching for Egypt some years ago I had a camel to help me – not a real-live camel, but a cut-out perched on top of a farm sign on the road to Aberdour Bay. The farmer who put it up, Joseph Gillanders, told me he had no idea why his farm was called Egypt, but he thought there might have been a gipsy encampment there at one time. Early in the eighteenth century the north-east was plagued by bands of vagabond Egyptians, or gipsies.

Another possibility is that the name had a Biblical origin. Egypt and Jericho were popular Biblical place names; the first name dates back to 1743 and Jericho at Culsalmond goes back to 1785. There is also a Pisgah in New Deer and a Mount Tabor in Strathdon.

This cut-out camel tops a sign pointing the way to Egypt – not the Egypt in the Middle East, but a farm near Aberdour Bay.

Place-name rhymes were once all the rage. This couplet, which apparently originated in Perth, gives a new twist to the mean Aberdonian story:

Old mannie Aberdeen
Sold his wifie for a peen.

Another piece of tightfisted marital trading involved Charles Leslie, better known as Mussel-mou'd Charlie, a poet and ballad singer who was known 'in every town and village from Rattray Head to the Firth of Forth'. He died at Old Rayne in 1782 at the age of 105. 'Oh dolefu' rings the bells o' Raine,' went a ballad written to mark his death, 'For Charlie ne'er will sing again.' It told of his wanderings 'through Angus, Buchan, Mearns and Mar' and said that in Edinburgh he bought a spouse 'for comfort of his life'. The price of his new wife was a bawbee – a half-penny:

Each ballad a bawbee him brought,
And for that sum his wife he bought,
Her tocher was not quite worth a plack,   *dowry; fourpence*
A farthing's worth of cut tobacco.

Mussel-mou'd Charlie Leslie, the packman poet, who bought a wife for a
bawbee – a half-penny – and had something left over to buy tobacco.

Charlie himself mentioned his marriage in one of his own ballads –

I bought a wife in Edinburgh
For a bawbee –
I got a farthing in again
To buy tobacco wi'.

THE
BALLAD BOOK.

MUSSEL MOU'D CHARLIE.

EDINBURGH:
MDCCCXXVII.

This Ballad Book carried a sketch of Mussel Mou'd Charlie, the poet and ballad singer known throughout Scotland.

Although Leslie placed little value on his new wife, others had kindlier thoughts about the 'weel faured' [well-favoured] lassies. An exile in Orkney, who yearned for his home-town, Aberdeen, wrote this:

I ken a toon, clean wa'ed and biggit weel,	*built*
Where the women's a' weel-faured and	
the men brave and leal,	
An' they ca' ilka een by a weel-kent name.	*each one*
An' when I ging to yon toon, I'm gangin'	*go*
to my hame.	
I ken a toon, it's gey grim an'auld,	*very*
It's biggit o' grey steen, an' some find it cauld.	
It's biggit up an' doon on hights beside the sea,	
But if I get to yon toon I'd bide there till I dee.	

Buchan not only said nice things about the ladies, but threw in a plug for their nowt and their swanky chiels:

Buchan for nowt, milk an' meal,	
Weel faured lass an' swanky chiel.	*smart chap*

One versifier was intent on getting the bonnie lassies away from Strathbogie:

The Bogie it is unco weet,	*extremely*
Gin' ye fa'in ye" weet yer feet,	*should you fall in*
So, bonnie lassie, come my road	
An' gang nae through the Bogie	

But there was a worse fate than getting your feet wet, for another verse gave advice to womenfolk on how to avoid an early grave:

If they wad drink nettles in March	
And eat Muggons in May,	
Sae many braw maidens	
Wadna gang to the clay.	*fine*

Like many place names and place-name rhymes, you get only half the story. There is nothing to indicate why so many maidens 'went to the clay'. Muggons are mugwort, a plant with aromatic leaves. I'm told that they are being sold today in herbal shops in the North-east.

From Fyvie came another health tip for both sexes:

Paul's wall an' Paul's water,
Drink ye this an' ye'll be better.

St Paul's Well is at Fyvie, a spring above Westerton, which was reckoned to have curative properties.

This reminds me of Wullie Gray's water. Wullie, a local farmer known as the Bard of Corgarff, opened up a well on his farm which he said provided the clearest, purest water you could get anywhere. He gave me a drink of it, then added some whisky, and told me about a woman from Swindon, Mrs Norah Coutts, who wrote a poem about it – the water, not the whisky. She called it 'Wullie's Water' and the first verse went:

'Twas clear as crystal, diamond bright,
An' tricklt ower ma lips,
It was a better drink by far
Than a' yer Hielan' nips.

Wullie, however, had strong opposition, for not far from his farm was a well called the Tobar Fuar, the Cold Well, which was supposed to have cured the blind, the lame and the deaf.

Weather was a subject that made place-name rhymsters reach for their pens. Long before round-the-clock weather forecasts were broadcast on television, a crofter could look at a hill and tell what lay in store. If it was raining over Morven, it would soon be pouring down on Cromar: 'When Morven hiz a tap, Cromar *'ll get a drap.*' On the other hand, if it was falling on Mormond – if the hill had 'put on its hat' – it was said that 'the Buchan howes would pay for that.' One version of the Morven rhyme said that 'Ladelick 'ill get a drap.'

The sea, roaring and grumbling off the North-east coast, also gave warnings of storms ahead. The following rhyme was often heard in the Pitsligo area:

Fin the rumble comes fae Pittendrum,   *when*
The ill weather's a' t' cum;
Fin the rumble comes fae Aberdour,
The ill weather's a' ower.   *all over*

There was another version which said that when the sea roared at Pittendrum 'the ill weather's tae come.' The 'rumble' came from the movement of stones in the sea, a noise which local folk heard quite clearly sitting in their houses. They regarded it as a reliable weather forecast. There was a similar weather verse from Macduff:

Fin the win' cums aff o' Cullycan
It's naither gude for baist nor man.'   *beast*

Cullycan is a headland to the east of the burgh.

But it wasn't all gloom on the weather front. The following was a couplet that many Moray farmers often heard:

A misty May and a dropping June
Brings the bonny land of Moray aboon.

The explanation for these lines is that much of Morayshire is of a sandy nature and the crops in May and June require a good deal of moisture to prevent them from becoming stunted.

A more ominous threat lies in the following lines:

Says Durie to Dorback.
'Where shall we sweep?'
'Through the middle o' Moy
When a' men sleep.'

Moy in Inverness-shire is the seat of the chiefs of Clan Mackintosh. The hamlet of Moy stands on the main north road to Inverness. The verse is a reference to the Muckle Spate of 1829, when swollen rivers like the Durie and Dorback swept through the countryside around Moy. It was there that a Hanoverian force was turned back when attempting to capture Prince Charles Stuart, who was sleeping at Moy Hall.

The Ugie, one of Buchan's great rivers, featured in a similar verse, although there was no Muckle Spate chasing its waters down to the sea:

Little Ugie said to Muckle Ugie,
'Where shall we meet?'
'Doon in the Haughs of Rora
When a man is asleep.'

The two streams that form the Ugie meet in the parish of Longside on the Haughs of Rora. Another version of the first line was 'Ugie said t' Ugie'.

Among the most puzzling of the place-name poems is a couplet about the Bridge of Dee in Aberdeen. It is said to have come from Leochel-Cushnie and it goes:

There's a wifie sits on the Brig o' Dee
An' aye she says, 'Gae me, gae me.'   *always; give*

There were a number of variations on this theme, one of which set out what the wife on the bridge *didn't* want:

| She wadna hae meal, she wadna hae maut, | *malt* |
| She wadna hae sugar, she wadna hae saut. | *salt* |

I have sometimes wondered if there was yet another version of the rhyme which told what happened to the 'Gae me, gae me' wife. The Brig o' Dee was a popular subject for place-name rhymsters. There was a verse about Willie Buck's coo, who seemed to have the same ambitions shown by the cow that jumped over the moon:

Willie Buck had a coo,	
Black and white about the moo,	*mouth*
They ca'd her Bell o' Blinty,	*called*
She jumpit ower the Brig o' Dee	
Like ony Covealintie.	*Covenanter*

Then there is the one about the Brig o' Dee farm servant who liked his brose:

Country Geordie, Brig o' Dee,
Sups his brose an' leaves the bree.

Willie Buck's coo could leap over the Bridge of Dee, but there was a cat that could do better than that. This is what was said about it:

| A cat could loup fae tree till tree, | *leap* |
| Fae Ballater to Corrachree. | |

Corrachree is an estate near Tarland. When I had a caravan at Tarland I often wandered over the Hill of Corrachree, crossing moorland riddled with the remains of stone circles. At one time, it was covered in woodland, as was much of the countryside, which was why 'a cat could loup fae tree till tree, fae Ballater to Corrachree'. The name itself bears witness to this, for Corrachree comes from the Gaelic *Coire chraobh,* 'the corrie of the trees'.

There was another two-liner which said much the same thing:

Fae Kilbirnie t' the sea
Ye may step fae tree till tree.

Kilbirnie is near the Ord, a few miles to the west of Banff. 'The rhyme indicates a very different state of matters in bygone days from what now exists,' said one writer. 'The tract of land at present between Kilbirnie and the sea is all under the plough and few trees are growing to adorn the landscape.'

The Devil, who often makes appearance in these old place-name rhymes, turns up in this verse:

The Pot o' Pittenyoul
Far the de'il gya the youl.   *Where the devil gives the howl*

The Pot o' Pittenyoul is a small pool in a stream called the Burn o' the Riggins, which flows past the village of Newmills of Keith. On the edge of the pool are some hollows worn away by the water and by stones and sand carried down by the stream. These hollows had the shape of a seat and it was said that Auld Nick sat down on the edge of the pool and left his mark.

The place-name writers came up with plenty of tongue-twisters. This was one from Banff about a poor man's mare:

The peer man's meer's deid,
The peer man's meer's deed,
Comin' fae Dundee,
The peer man's meer's deid,
Faht ailt the breet t' dee?   *What ailed tre brute*
It took the gut, the graivel,
The sturdy an' the staivel,
That ailt the breet t' dee.

There is also this verse from a Mrs Malcolm, Leochel-Cushnie, which appears to be a nonsense poem:

As I gaed up my humfue jump,
My humfue jumpie javie,
And there I saw Jahoca-poca
    carry away Gipangie.
Gin I had had my tick my tack
My tick my tack my tangie
I widna laten Jahoca-poca
    Carry away Gipangie.

The answer to this puzzle is that it describes a wolf carrying off a sheep. Work it out if you can!

3

CUSHNIE CAUL

At Cushnie Caul	
I bigget my faul,	*built; sheepfold*
At Ininteer	
I simmered my steer;	*cattle*
At Little Lynturk	
I drew my durk;	*dirk*
At Baldieven	
I stack it in.	

That old place-rhyme became a route map to me when I had a caravan at Tarland some years ago. I came to know 'Cushnie Caul' well and to feel the raw winds that gave it its name. In time, I tracked down the other places in the verse, from the oddly-named Ininteer (or Eninteer) to the mysterious Baldieven.

A range of low hills dominates the skyline behind Tarland, separating Leochel-Cushnie (Cushnie Caul) from the Howe of Cromar. This hill mass is generally known by the name of its highest peak, Pressendye, but the Ordnance Survey map shows other hills scattered along the ridge. These include Pittenderrich (the town of the foal) and Mally Watt (the long hill). The OS map shows the latter as Molly Watt's Hill, but the place-name expert William M. Alexander bluntly dismissed this as 'quite wrong'. Then, on the north side of the range, there is Ben na Flog, which Alexander described as having 'a pimple-like protuberance on its profile'.

The Gaels put it more succinctly. It was, they said, *beinn phloc* or *a' phluic* – 'the hill of the pluke'.

I came to know the Pressendye ridge very well, tramping along a track that was once used by drovers pushing their cattle on to markets in the south. I always took as my starting point the Lazy Well, which is shown on the OS map. When I found it there were half a dozen cans of beer cooling in it, no doubt put there by thirsty fishers. Near the well, which lies at the foot of Ballochbuie Hill – *bealach buie,* the yellow pass – is an old track called the Lazywell Road. This road, which crossed the watershed at its lowest point and pushed on to Strathdon, was known as the yellow pass in the days when it was the most used hill crossing going north from Cromar. It can still be followed today, running down past three lochans called the Lazy Well lochs. Less than a mile to the east, between the *Lazywell* Road and Pressendye, another track provided a direct route from Tarland to Towie, crossing Mally Watt Hill.

From the Pressendye ridge you look out on a spider's web of old tracks, across a vast panorama of hill country and farmland, north to the Hill of Coilliebhar. I climbed Coillebhar, not because it is a great height (it isn't

The Lazy Well lochs.

much more than 1,000ft), but because Donside folk had built a monster bonfire there to celebrate Queen Victoria's Jubilee. It was from Coilliebhar that I went south in search of 'Stachie' Laing, an eccentric chapman who had written *Donean Tourist.*

I was looking for the Rumblie Burn, which gurgled past an old kirkyard that had been one of 'Stachie's' haunts. He grubbed around old grave-stones looking for unusual epitaphs, which he subsequently published. Fighting shoulder-high nettles and willowherbs, dodging weed-strewn tombstones, I struggled in vain to find the sort of crude epitaph that would have delighted 'Stachie,' like one about the man who 'lived like a hog and died like a dog'. The best I could come up with was an inscription which read, 'Here lies the dust of the late James Leslie . . .'

From the north, Leochel-Cushnie can be reached by a maze of back roads skirting Colliebhar Hill and taking you through countryside where crofts and cottar houses look as if they have remained unchanged since 'Stachie' Laing knocked at their doors, squinting at the cottar wives with his 'gleyd' eye.

When I set out to rediscover Leochel-Cushnie, I had as my guide a Stirling man, George Williams, who wrote about the area in 1864. I never discovered what his connection was with the north-east, or with Leochel-Cushnie, but he wrote four articles in *Scottish Notes and Queries* under the title 'Notes on the Place Names of Leochel Cushnie.' He knew every farm, croft, kirk, smiddy, burn, mill, bog and well. He could tell you about the wood of the Warlock's Well, about a pool between Cushnie and Towie on top of a hill known as Plausie's Peel, about the Caul' Wall between Cushnie House and Milltown, and about the Four and Twenty Puddock well at Kirk-hill. The last name caught my fancy, but I was never able to trace the well – or the puddocks [frogs].

These names come creeping out of old maps and documents to tease the onomastics enthusiast. George Williams unearthed a wealth of them in his Leochel-Cushnie travels, 'slochter,' for instance, a marvellous word to describe very damp ground, and the Thundery Burn, where a small stream was turned into a raging spate 'by some terrible thunder.' One that caught my eye was Foggieley, which indicated bad husbandry. It made me wonder if bad husbandry gave Aberchirder its nickname – Foggieloan – but, in fact, it got its nickname because it was built on mossy land.

Williams also mentions the Drinkin' Pots at the source of the Thief's Burn. The cateran who came raging over the hills to Deeside and Donside must have quenched their thirst there, among them the infamous Gilderoy and Dhugair. This was the way they made their inroads on Cushnie and Corse.

In the late eighteenth century, William Forbes of Corse, whose house was plundered by the cateran, vowed: 'If God spares my life I shall build a house at which thieves will knock ere they enter.' But nothing could halt these wild Highlanders. John Dugar (John Dow McGregor) was one of the most notorious of the 'lawless byke of infamous thieves and limmers' who descended on Cushnie and Corse in the early years of the seventeenth century. 'He wald tak thair horss, ky and oxin,' wrote the historian John Spalding, 'and caus the owneris compone and pay for thair owin geir. He troublet the merchandis at Bartholomew fair and causit thame to pay soundlie.'

On one occasion, Dugar went to the Laird of Corse's lands and 'took out ane brave gentilman tennant', George Forbes, who was dwelling there. He then got word to the laird to send him a ransom of one thousand pounds – the amount paid by the Secret Council for the taking of Gilderoy. If the money wasn't forthcoming, said Dugar, he would 'send his manis heid to him'. Forbes was later released without ransom.

There is a farm called Bogside, east of Leochel-Cushnie, which Dugar raided in 1639. He and his accomplices took Alexander Forbes 'out of his owne houss in Bogsyde', bound his hands, and released him later for 'ane certain soume of money'. Dugar, according to Spalding, did 'gryt skaith' to the name of Forbes, and to the lairds of Corse, Leslie, Craigievar, and 'some others'. Dugar and his men abused their bounds, plundered their horses, cattle, sheep, goods and gear, 'because they were the instruments of Gilderoy, thair friend's death'.

The gloomy remains of Corse Castle, which William Forbes built to hold back the cateran, loom darkly out of the trees above the Corse Burn. It was raised in a strong position, with its walls pierced by gun-loops and shot-holes and tiny diamond-shaped windows which were probably used for defence. The entrance is in the foot of the square tower, where a lintel carried the initials W.F. for William Forbes and E.S. for Elizabeth Strachan his wife, dated 1581. Now the interior is completely gutted and it is difficult to trace much of the lay-out.

Echoes of that violent past were in my mind when I made my way to Leochel-Cushnie, up past Cauldhame (see Chapter 4), Bogfern, Dunsdyke, Confunderland and the road to Wark. The name Wark strikes discordant chords. The farm of Wark is an undistinguished building, although it was dignified back in 1600 as the Wark o' Cushnie. It is unusual to see the name applied to a farm. Macdonald said it was usually given to a castle or other large building.

George Williams says that mills furnished a considerable number of the place-names of Leochel-Cushnie. He named some of them: Mill of Brux, Milton of Cairncoullie, Mill of Ininteer ('At Ininteer, I simmered my steer'), Caigmill, Mill of Fowlis, Lady Mill, which is thought to have been called after the grandmother of Lord Sempill, Milton of Course, and Waukmill. (There were some two dozen wauk mills where cloth was thickened and felted by soaking, beating and shrinking). The Mill of Cushnie had arms above the door. There was also a Claymill, which, like many other houses, may have been built of heather and dubs [muds].

There is a seasaw ride from the Tarland road to the Towie road. On the way up there is a farm called Craigiestep across the fields on the left. Williams says the name 'arose from the steep descent on the road going to Tarland.' After the turn-off to Wark farm you come to Brae Smith Garage (there is also a Brae Smithy croft). The word 'brae' is particularly appropriate because here you drop steeply down to Milton of Cushnie, giving you a lovely view of the Howe of Cushnie.

I turned left at a T-junction and just round the corner, set back off the road, was a house with a stone saying 'Post Office 1870'. It had been a shop as well as a Post Office and a metal sign on the wall said 'Telephone'. Well, all that was in the good old days. Shirley Maycock came to the door of the house. She arrived at Cushnie in 1986, all the way from Croydon. She didn't carry on the P.O., but kept the shop going for four years. There is no phone there now. Shirley said she just hadn't got around to taking the sign down.

I climbed away from the Howe, up a steep road past the farm of Balchimmy, and down to join the Towie road. I was looking for the place where the little people live – Elfhillock. Elves, says the dictionary, are 'small, manlike and mischievous', and tradition has it that they frequented the farm of Elfhillock. William Alexander said that although it was Elfhillock on the map, Elphin was the name of the farm and the Elfhillock was beside it.

There was another entry on Elphin, linked with Ellon and Aberdour, and throwing cold water on the myths of the 'little people'. It said that although Elphin or Elfin was often interpreted as elf-hill, the name was Gaelic, probably *ailbhinn,* a rock. Also, there was an odd protruding rock on the hilltop near Ellon, above the summit of the old Aberdeen to Deer road, and at Aberdour the name Elphin was attached to the top end of New Aberdour village.

Shirley Maycock at Milton of Cushnie. She came north to Cushnie in 1986 and ran the shop there for four years.

Elves and fairies kept popping up in place-name literature in the old days. This place-name rhyme had an elf in it:

Bleary, Buckie, Backie, Jackie,
The East Toon, the West Toon,
The Quithel an Pitwathum,
Annamuck and Elfhill,
The Gowans an the Tannachie.

Some of these are contractions – Bleary is Blairerno, Buckie is Buckiesmill, and Jackie is Jacksbank. You can still find these names in the Glenbervie area.

Undeterred by the doubters, I continued my search for the wee folk. I couldn't find the track to Elfhillock and landed up at the nearby farm of Hillockhead. The farmer, Alan Marshall, breeds pedigree Aberdeen-Angus cattle. He came from Croydon. He hadn't heard any stories about fairies, but, pointing up the hill, he said there was an old ruin there with a curious name.

I eventually found Elfhillock and discovered that the farmer was Lloyd Fowlie, an electrician I had met when he was working in Glenbuchat. He had taken over the farm four years ago. He was living in a big, impressive wooden house, which he had extended. The old farmhouse was across the yard and Lloyd had converted it and the steading into stables.

He had heard about the fairies story. He pointed up the hill to the ruin that Alan Marshall had mentioned. I could just pick it out near the top of the hill. The name was on the map: Beadshallock, a name that might conjure up thoughts of elves and fairies. The ruins lay in the shadow of Beadshallock Hill and Lloyd said that before the area was afforested a road ran over the hill and down to Cushnie, providing a useful short-cut to people going from the Towie side.

Bead is given in the Scots Dictionary as an alternative to 'bede,' so it might have been a Bede House [almshouse]. The dictionary says that 'shalloch' means abundant, but Bigieshalloch was from *Bob seilich*, a willow bog. There were other ruins farther over the hill. Not far from Beadshalloch was Ben-na-Flog: the pluke hill.

Lloyd Fowlie at Elfhillock, a farm where the
wee folk were said to live.

Before we left, Lloyd asked if we knew where the hillock was. We didn't. It was down at the bottom of the farm track, covered in trees. Parts of a dyke could be seen around it. But there were no fairies – so we left. Nevertheless, I couldn't help thinking of what George Williams had said about Elfhillock. He told of how at the beginning of the nineteenth century a young man pulled 'a birn' of heather on Elfhillock and carried it to his aunt at Hillockhead – Alan Marshall's farm.

'The women were baking,' writes Williams, 'and under ordinary circumstances his services would have been appreciated; but, on telling them where he got the heather he was straightaway ordered to go and replace it carefully, that his foolhardy conduct might not enrage the elves that kept court there.' It was said that a man spent 'a year and a day' there and thought it was only an hour or two at the most.

Another tale about the Elfhillock was that, though it was a small knoll, a noise, however loud, made on one side, could not be heard on the other side; and a cry, however shrill, uttered at the foot, could not be heard at the top. Williams says that he tried the experiment 'twenty or thirty years ago', which would have been about 1860–70. It didn't work and Williams was 'disgusted to find that the hillock had lost its virtue'.

So that was that. I left the 'little people' and headed back along the

Elfhillock – the fairy hillock, at the start of the track to the farm.

Towie road. I was looking for the second farm in my Cushnie Caul verse: Eninteer. The name means the carpenter's brae, but at some future time people may call it the hammer thrower's brae, for the man I went to see at Eninteer was Henry Gray, the great 'heavy' of Highland Games, who first broke the heavy hammer record at Aboyne Games in 1953.

Eninteer stands on a brae above the Cushnie Burn. I had come to the conclusion that half the population of Leochel Cushnie lived on hills or braes. George Williams netted a bagful of them in his articles – the Brae into Milton of Cushnie, Braehead and Drybraes, and the intriguing *Leadhlich*, 'the hillside of flagstones'. Peasiewhins, a type of stone, usually granite, were quarried there.

Then there was Lynturk, one of my place-rhyme farms, whose name meant the boar's pool, but *Ledyntuyrk*, as it was known in 1407, meant the boar's braeside.

Henry Gray's braeside farm is a mile west of Muir of Fowlis. The farm track ran down to the Cushnie Burn, where a frail-looking bridge took us over the water, then climbed up to West Eninteer farm, with a second track

Henry Gray, the great Games 'heavy' of yesteryear.

breaking away to East Eninteer. Henry was outside in his yard, a tall, grizzled veteran in his seventies; he looked as if he could chuck a hammer or throw a caber with as much ease as he had done half a century ago.

We sat at his fireside and talked. I told him about the place-name rhyme with Eninteer in it, but he had never heard of it. He knew about crofters 'simmering their steers' in the summer, but thought that had gone on farther up Strathdon. I said I'd give him another place-name rhyme: the Tillyorn verse (see Chapter 4).

'Aye!' he said when I was finished. He'd heard of Tillyorn putting through the corn and Wester Corse the straw, but he had never heard about Cauldhame having 'naething ava'.

'It must have been an Englishman that was there,' I joked, and told him about the Coldhome at Migvie.

He laughed. 'It's an Englishman that's in West Eninteer.'

There have been six generations of Grays at Eninteer. George was born there and, he says, has been there 'a' my days'. His uncle George was a policeman and Henry had all the attributes needed to become a bobby – 6ft 6in of brawn and muscle. He recalls that when anyone from the police came to Eninteer his mother would say, 'Tak' that loon in an' pit him intae the bobbies.'

Uncle George didn't encourage it. 'Better nae!' he said.

Henry Gray's farm at Eninteer.

Instead, his strength and energy, sharpened by hard farm work, went into making a name for himself in the world of the 'heavies.' The first time he went in for competitive hammer-throwing was at the Craigievar estate picnic in 1947. He won first prize. When he competed at the Tarland show a couple of years later he was told that Lady MacRobert of Douneside wanted to see him. She was patron of the Aboyne Games and wanted him to compete there. She asked if he had a kilt and when he said 'No' she told him to go to the Tarland tailor and have one made. She would pay for it.

He became friendly with George Clark, who was a big name in the games world. George gave him advice and encouragement and they often practised together at Eninteer. 'He was a bit o' a worthy', recalled Henry. 'There was a bit o' humour about him.'

In 1953, Henry decided to go in for a competition run by the Spartan Club in the Music Hall, Aberdeen. The show featured the famous Dinnie stones, which Donald Dinnie had carried from one side of the Potarch Bridge to the other. In the Spartan Club contest the idea was to carry one stone across the stage, a distance of twenty yards. Henry prepared himself by tying four 56-lb weights together and carrying them around the loft in his steading. He dropped the stone two yards short of the goal, but he got his prize of £20. He spent it on a new coat.

The games are not what they were. 'They've a' changed a bit', said Henry. 'They're a' oot for the money noo.' His days of throwing the hammer and tossing the caber are over, but he still judges at some of the games. I took my leave of this friendly giant and bumped my way down the farm track and over the Cushnie Burn.

There were two farms in the verse I still had to see – Little Lynturk and Baldieven. I had been unable to find Baldieven on any map or place-name book, but Henry said there was a Baldyvin near Alford.

I wanted to find out why the Cushnie Caul poet had been sticking a dirk into someone, but I was tempted away by the thought of refreshment at the Muggerthaugh Inn, which was only half a mile away. Its name has always intrigued me. Williams, writing about the carpenter's braeside, said that another useful man in the community was the mugger, or capper. In the old times, according to Macdonald, a mugger was a maker of wooden dishes.

I ended my journey in the shadow of Craigievar Hill. There is a curious story about the farm of Mowatseat, on the west side of the hill. It is said that the last Mowat of Fowlis wanted to be buried 'beyond sight of kirk or mill'. The funeral procession had reached 'a little mound overgrown with grass, called Mowat's Seat', when the corpse suddenly became so heavy that the bearers had to stop and bury the coffin there – out of sight of church or mill.

George Williams gives another explanation of this spooky happening. He says that Mowat Seat marks the place where the whisky began to take effect on the carriers of Mowat's coffin, and that was where they rested it. But my hunt for place-names ended at a spot whose name seemed to put a crown on my stravaiging in Leochel-Cushnie. The fields near Mowat Seat were known at one time as the Backwairds of Craigievar. The servants at Craigievar Castle had their own name for it, which I liked. They called it 'the back o' God's elbow'.

4

CAULDHAME

Tillyorn grow the corn,
Wester Corse, the straw,
Tillylodge, the blawart blae,   *bluebell*
Cauldhame, naething ava.   *at all*

The words of the old jingle were dirlin' in my head when I turned off the
Tarland road and headed over the hills to Leochel Cushnie. The fields
of Tillyorn and Wester Corse were on my right, Tillylodge was behind me,
and up in front I could see a sign at the end of a farm track – Cauldhame.

The icy North-east winds seem to have blown up a storm of 'Cauld' place-
names over the years. The first 'Cauld' farm I ever stayed on was my uncle's
farm near New Byth, but that was Cauldwells, where there was a dam, but no
well. There was a Cauldmoss at Peterhead and Cauldhames at Keig and
Tarland. There was even a Cauldsowens at Fyvie – a whimsical name, said
William Alexander. (Sowens is a dish of steeped and fermented oats.)

Cauldhame was by far the most popular name. Others have disappeared, but Cauldhame can still be found on Ordnance Survey maps. It
has been around for a long time, for records show that it was in use as far
back as 1696.

But names change. Tillyorn, *tulach eorn,* barley knoll, was originally
Knowhead and earlier versions of the verse gave the line: 'Blackbank, the
blawart blae.' Blawart is the Scots word for harebell, best known to most
folk as the bluebell.

Tarland, the village which was once known for its 'Tarland tykes'.

The sign at Cauldwells Farm, Turriff, where the author spent his holidays as a boy.

Why Cauldhame got such a bad name is a mystery. There were worse names. But an explanation of the Cauldhame at Tillylodge can be found in the Slack of Tillylodge, a well-known cut between the hills. An earlier name for it was Clasnage, *Clais nan gaoth*, 'the windy ravine'. This stretch of country off the Tarland road throws up some intriguing names. Not far from Tillylodge is Tillyorn, where they 'grow the corn,' and to the east of it is the oddly-named Tillyskukie. The proper name is Tillyskuke, but locals always called it 'Skookie'. 'Tilly' means knoll and there is a rash of them in Aberdeenshire. Tillycroy, east of 'Skookie,' comes from *Tulach cruaidh*, 'hard knoll'. Farther east, up a muddy farm track almost opposite the Crossroads Hotel, is Futtiepark. The word Futtie is the same as Footie, which means foot of the hill or low ground. There is a Futtie Stripe at Rayne, a stripe being a small stream.

Names like Cauldhame and Frostybrae are described by place-name experts as 'jocular names', but whether or not the farm workers who lived there saw the funny side of it is another matter. James Macdonald says they belonged to 'the old-time sarcastic names of farms.' They were a kind of protest poetry, crying out against poor working conditions and against tight-fisted farmers and their carping wives. A grace from Leochel-Cushnie spoke about the 'deil and sorrow' dished out by one farmer's wife:

The Cauldhame farm sign near the Tarland road.

The roadside sign to Tillyskukie ('Skookie').

The road to Futtiepark.

Thin brose and nae breid,
Oh, God, gin she were deid.

Another verse on the same theme – all work and no play – went:

Doon in Nether Dallachy,
There's neither watch nor clock,
But dinner time and supper time
An' aye yoke, yoke.   *begin work*

Bakebare, Thirstyhillock, Frostyhill, Frosty Nib (on Mormond Hill), Hadagain, Wealthy Town, Peeledegg, Warldsend . . . these were names which Macdonald marked down as unproductive land. The doggerel describing them, he said, was current in Aberdeenshire in the seventeenth century. There was a Hadagain at Midmar and Macdonald said he had no doubt that it was a humorous name indicating that the farm or croft was considered very bad land, unprofitable and difficult to work. There was a public house between Woodside and Bucksburn and the name is still there today.

Peeledegg doesn't seem to quite fit the picture, It formerly meant something like 'a stroke of luck' or 'a windfall'. Warldsend was the name of a house in both Tarves and Fraserburgh in the eighteenth century. The Tarves building was dated 1751 and the Fraserburgh house was said to be 'at the south end of the shore, 1728, tenement commonly called the Drinnie or Worles End'.

The world hadn't come to an end when I was tramping down the old Buchan railway line to Maud a few years ago. A rutted farm track crossed the line near Maud and, nailed to a tree, was a wooden sign saying, 'World's end'. The next time I went that way the sign had gone and I wondered why it had been removed, for although it was a small farm it had been dignified by a place in the Ordnance Survey maps.

It was from a Maud woman, Mrs M. Panton, a farmer's wife, that I was given a number of old field names at the Mains of Clackriach. They were Frostyhill, Frostybrae and Scrapehard, the last one being, she said, 'very aptly named'. The Panton family had been at Clackriach since 1901 and used the field names all the time. Clackriach itself came from *Glac riabhach*, 'the grey coloured ravine'. The old Castle of Clackriach and the Mains stand in the 'glack' (a hollow or a ravine) to which the name refers.

'Bakebare' was another name indicating unproductive ground. What the name really means has never been clear, but one theory is that it had something to do with bere meal (barley meal) and that the farm workers didn't like their cakes made with it.

There is a couplet that goes:

Bakebare and Brewthin
Claa the Wa'as and Clickumin.

There was said to be a Bakebare in Drumoak. Here, from the Cullerlie crossroads, a narrow back road cuts through to the North Deeside road. It was once a busy highway used by horse and cattle dealers – coupers – on their way to the trysts and fairs in the north-east and today it is still used as a short-cut to the Deeside road.

It was called the Couper's Road and it was fed by traffic coming north by the old Mounth passes and crossing the Dee by the ford at the Mills of Drum. This was where Edward I, the Hammer of the Scots, crossed the river after staying at Durris Castle in 1296 and it was here, too, that Montrose crossed with his army of Irishmen and wild Highlanders in 1644 before descending on Aberdeen.

It is a dream world for place-name addicts. On the way down from Cullerlie a farm track branches off to Quiddies Mill, where Dugald Macpherson has lived for fourteen years. 'Quiddies,' he told me, was an old Scots word for sheepfold. At one time there had been a flax mill there and the weavers who worked at it had lived in a settlement whose ruins lay in a nearby field.

Beyond Quiddies was Candiglerach, or Candyglearach, one of the ancient lands of the Forest of Drum. The name comes from *Ceann-de-Clearch,* 'head of the clerk, or clergyman'.

There were other curious names . . . Murphy Howe, or Murpie Howe, which was even more confusingly pronounced 'Murfy Howe'; and there was Quartains, which had once been a desolate moor, and a farm called Horsewells, a reminder of the days of the coupers.

So on it went – signposts to the past – but the name I was looking for, Bakebare, was nowhere to be seen. I wondered if it had been changed over the years, as many place names were, and I remembered what George Williams had written in his Leochel-Cushnie notes. He said that at the farm of Culmellie there were 'parks at the gate o' the hoose and back o' the hoose', and west on the same side of the burn were the Bogfauld, Cots Parkie, and Begbare. Not Bakebare, *Beg*bare. The last name reminded him of the rhyme:

The farm of Quiddiesmill lies off the Couper's Road
at Drumoak. Quiddies is an old Scots word for sheepfold
and at one time there was a flax mill there.
Its ruin lie in a nearby field.

This sign is on the Couper's Road. The name Candyglirach (there are
different spellings) marks the ancient lands of the Forest of Drum. It comes
from *Ceann-de-Clerach*, 'head of the clerics, or clergyman', and is pronounced
'Canny-glerich'.

Begbare and Brew thin,
Claw the wa's o Cleekumin.

Names beginning with 'Beg' generally meant a bog, as in Begshill in
Drumblade, which was formerly Bogshill, and Bogeshill in 1693. In the
mid-seventeenth century the low ground at Drumblade was bog; peat was
cut on land that was later cultivated. There was a Begsburn at Echt, but
when I went to see it the name had changed to Strathburn.

The likelihood, then, was that Bakebare had originally been Begbare, and
that the name simply meant a bare bog and not the barley meal that made
farmer lads turn up their noses. Oddly enough, it was near Begsburn that I
found the answer to another name in the Bakebare couplet – Brewthin.

This was the name of a farm near Garlogie, not far from what was
Begsburn. According to Jamieson's Scottish Dictionary, the word 'brew'
meant soup or broth, so it may be that some farmer's wife was serving up
thin broth as well as thin brose and nae breid.

Peter Sinclair, who has farmed at Brewthin for thirty years, had never
heard this story. He thought, like a lot of other people, that there had been
an inn named Brewthin at one time, but the link with Cleikumin threw
doubt on that because Cleikumin was supposed to be the name of an inn.
It is said that it got its name because innkeepers tried to cleek (grab or
clutch) their customers in to the hostelry. There is, incidentally, a
Cleikhimin Pot at Towie, a fine fishing pool on the Don, and the name
there refers to the hooking and drawing in of fish.

Both Macdonald and Alexander dismiss the inn theory, and both plump for
Cleikhimin as a farm. Macdonald drew attention to a farm at Lumphanan that
was called Cleikumin until some unimaginative farmer changed it to Hillhead.
There was also a Cleikumin along with the Cleikum Moor at Loch Davan.

'Cla' the wa's' is the final mystery in the Bakebare jingle. At one time there
was a farm instrument called a claut, a scraper with a long handle used to
clean the byre of dung. Peter Sinclair hadn't heard of such a thing, but thought
it was what he called a 'creper', which was used for hauling dung out of a cart.
Jamieson's entry on creepers reads, 'Creparis. Grapels of iron. Creepers.'

When I was researching the place names and place rhymes of the north-
east, they seemed to mirror a life of sweated labour, poor food and poverty.
But not all farms in the place rhymes were like that. There was one place
that stood out from the rest – Wealthytown. It was given in both place-
name books, but no explanation of the name accompanied it. I set out to
find the answer.

5

WEALTHY TOWN

I was driving along the road to Keig, with the familiar Mither Tap frowning down at me from across the moors. I was thinking of the lines from one of Charles Murray's poems, recalling how he had wandered over these hills with a friend: 'Up Nochtyside or throu' the Cabrach braes, Doon the Lord's Throat an' ootower Bennachie.' It reminded me of a joke that was well known in the area. When visitors asked how they could get to Paradise they were told 'Doon the Lord's Throat.'

This Paradise, however, was an earthly one – the famous Paradise Woods, planted over two centuries ago by Sir Archibald Grant of Monymusk. The Lord's Throat was a road named after Lord Forbes of Castle Forbes, although strictly speaking it should have been *My* Lord's Throat.

Like 'Hamewith', I went down the Lord's Throat, but not 'ootower Bennachie.' Nochtyside and the Cabrach braes could wait for another time. Instead, I was heading for a huddle of houses where the Lord's Throat ends. This was Keig – and the people who lived there thought that *they* were in Paradise. Standing in Sheena Lyon's lounge, I looked out over a breathtaking panorama. Sheena, who has been there since 1995, never tires of it; the space, the changing seasons, the riot of colour – you never get used to it, she said. She had just built a big conservatory so that she could get an even better view.

I had come to Keig looking for a place called 'Wealthytown'. I had seen the name in a place-name book, but there were no details, nothing to show how it got such a name. I had heard of farms with despairing place names.

People wrote poems about such places, but nobody ever wrote about wealthy *touns,* unless it was to tilt at tight-fisted farmers and their frugal wives. Was there really such a place as Wealthytown?

I had never been in Keig and knew little about it, but I remembered the name from a well-known verse called 'The Travelling Preacher.'

> Up to Tough an' doon by Towie
> Gaed the wife and her bowie: *barrel*
> Through by Keig and Tullynessle
> 'Twas aye the wifie and her vessel:
> Up Glenbuchat and Strathdon
> Still he drave the wifie on:
> Syne hame by Rhynie and Strathbogie   *since*
> Cam' the wifie and her cogie.   *wooden vessel*

I knew all the places that the wifie and her cogie had been, except Keig. I was encouraged by the fact that it featured in 'The Travelling Preacher', but less impressed when I read what Alexander Smith had to say about Keig parish in *A New History of Aberdeenshire* in 1875. He wrote, 'It has neither towns nor villages, neither has it any very remarkable curiosities.' As for the name of the parish, William M. Alexander gave it short shrift in his *Place-names of Aberdeenshiure*. All he said was that Keig rhymed with 'vague'. It sounded like the old whisky advertisement, 'Don't be Vague, ask for Keig'.

On the other hand, James Macdonald, in his *Place Names of West Aberdeenshire,* had some intriguing ideas about its origin. He believed that it was a personal name, as it was in Ireland, and he pointed out that Keige and Keig were common names on the Isle of Man. Nearer to home, he said that Mackeggie was a Scottish form of the name. I wondered if he thought that kilted Mackeggies had come tramping over Bennachie and down the Lord's Throat to build a settlement and call it Keig. Maybe they had. Mary Pettrie, former head teacher of Keig School, told me she had seen the name Keggie on an old map dating back to 1824.

It was Wealthytown that had a hold over me – I was haunted by that irresistible name. The first time I went to Keig I saw a sign over a gate saying 'Wealthiton Croft'. The croft had gone and the house was now just one of a straggle of buildings on the road to Montgarrie. The school was near it. It had two classrooms, fifteen pupils in each, and three staff members, two full time. The pupils were given different projects and I thought they might have done one on Wealthytown, but they hadn't. Perhaps they will take up the challenge sometime.

Wealthiton Croft at Old Keig.

The Wealthiton sign at the roadside.

There was, incidentally, a girls' school in Keig at one time and also a Free Church school.

There had been a Post Office and a shop at the west end of the village, where the row of houses runs out. Both shop and P.O. have gone, although there is still a sign saying 'Post Office'. Behind this is Wealthyton Cottage, the home of Valerie Morris, one of the teachers. I came across an OS map which showed Wealthyton House next to the P.O. It turned out that this was the house attached to the shop. The occupant was William Miller, whose father, Dave Miller, came down from Orkney to take over the shop when he bought it in 1963. When he retired in 1987 the shop closed.

His son, who works in Aberdeen, couldn't shed light on the mystery of the Wealthytown name, but he passed on a bit of scandalous gossip that had drifted down the years. This was that the house was built in 1927 for some gentleman's 'bidie-in'. A woman living with a man when not married to him. I asked another resident if she had heard that story. She said, 'no', but then added, 'I could believe it'. The shop was built after the 'bidie-in' had gone. It was later turned into a tea-blending centre. Some of the Wealthytown cottages are said to have been built for the tea-blending employees.

The Millers ran the shop as an old-fashioned country store, catering for all needs. It was basically a licensed grocer, but it was also a drapery, sold hen foods and fancy goods and had the Post Office. Before the Millers' time a van from the shop went out and about the countryside.

Willie Miller said that Keig had changed over the years. 'There were hardly any houses here when we came,' he said. Now there are smart modern houses in Keig's one and only street. There was a smiddy at the other end of the village, but it was knocked down to make way for two new houses. The feeling in the village is that it should have been made a listed building and saved from demolition.

The oldest couple in Keig are Sandy Mitchell and his wife Ann. Sam, now retired, is in his late seventies. They have been in their house at 2 Atholl Cottages for forty-eight years. If anyone knew about the origin of Wealthytown it should have been Sandy and his wife, but, no, they couldn't help me.

Olive Fraser, who lives in the west end of the villlage, said that the previous owner of her house, which was built in 1927, had changed the name. It was originally called Wealthytown Cottage; now it is called Marchmont. Olive, with an all-embracing wave of her arm, said, 'This was *all* Wealthytown.' In a sense, Wealthytown was like an old farm *toun*. Farm *touns* were groups of houses, units of eight or nine townships, with tenants, sub-tenants and cottars with a house but no land. Many of the *touns* had weavers, and souters, tailors and knitters, catering for the communities. For instance, in Monymusk, which lies at the other end of the Lord's Throat, there were twenty-four such townships.

The 1851 census for Keig was interesting. There were seven separate houses under the name Wealthitown (note the spelling). The first house on the list had seventeen people living in it. The head of the house was Alexander Bruce, whose occupation was given as general merchant and farmer (180 acres). He had a wife, Agnes, three daughters and five sons. He also had three farm servants and a girl servant called Elizabeth. There were a number of visitors staying with the Bruces. One was a nephew, Charles Bruce, who was listed as an M.A. of King's College, Aberdeen; also George Copland, a farmer, and Adam Stephen, a cattle dealer.

The other houses had only a handful of people in them. They were probably cottar houses. There was a variety of occupations: labourer and sexton, a farmer with six acres of ground, a shopkeeper, a merchant, a cattle dealer, a knitter, a carpenter – all in little Keig. There was also the school.

Mary Petrie, who was head teacher of the school for twenty-one years (she retired fifteen years ago) put forward a theory about the Wealthytown mystery. She thought that the better-off people had lived in the west end of the village, while the less well-off lived in the east end. When I mentioned this to Olive Fraser, she said that on one occasion a minister had said from the pulpit that even if the wealthier folk lived in the west end they were no better than those in the east end.

The folk of Keig were friendly and helpful, but at the end of my search the big questions still remained unanswered – who gave Wealthytown its name, and why? I decided that there was only one person who could help me – the Laird. Castle Forbes, originally called Putachie, is about half a mile east of the village. It is the seat of the Lords Forbes, premier barons of Scotland, but it is not an atttractive building. The author Nigel Tranter said it was 'scarcely beautiful, though the setting is fine.' The sharp-tongued Lord Cockburn, in his *Circuit Journeys,* was less restrained. He thought it was 'in as bad taste as possible.' He wondered that the building 'did not tremble lest the true old castles of this most architectural shire should step out and tread his base tower and contemptible bright freestone under their feet.'

The present Lord Forbes, however, no longer lives in the castle. His son, Malcolm, the Master of Forbes, has taken over the running of the estate and with his wife Jinny runs the castle as a private guest house. Lord Forbes has moved into a house on the estate and renamed it Balforbes – Forbes' town. I found him walking up the drive to his house, using a thumb-stick. He looked frail, but was friendly and easy to talk to. He said he had read my book, *Land of the Lost.* He was particularly interested in the chapter on Monymusk and the planting of Sir Archibald Grant's woodland, which was described in one eighteenth-century map as the Garden of Paradise. I told him about my efforts to find the origins of the name Wealthytown and about the theory that it had been called that because it was in the west end of the village. He agreed that it was possible. Did he himself know any explanation for the name? He hesitated, then said, a little ruefully I thought, 'I don't know'.

So that was the end of my search for the secret of Wealthytown. Before I left Keig I had one more place to visit – Old Keig. When I was with Mary Petrie she took me to the back of her house and pointed across the fields to a belt of trees in the distance, and to Old Keig Farm, which was near it. Alexander Smith wrote in his *New History of Aberdeenshire* that Keig didn't have any 'very remarkable curiosities'. No one could have told him about the stone circle at Old Keig.

Robbie Mortimer farms at Old Keig, following in his father's footsteps. He had been up at four o'clock in the morning, but he dropped what he was doing and took me to the stone circle. Crossing a field towards it, he pointed to high ground to the north. Here, at 930 feet, was another 'curiosity' not mentioned by Alexander Smith – the Barmekin, a circular hilltop fort 220 feet in diameter. Unfortunately, no one could see the fort because the hill had been planted over with trees.

The Keig stones have been called Stones of Wonder. I could see why as I approached the circle and saw its huge recumbent crouched in the belt of trees like some sleeping monster. The experts say it is the largest known. It is 16 feet long by six feet high and five feet broad at one end – and it weighs no less than 53 tons. Two upright stones stand nine feet above the ground and the recumbent is placed so that the midwinter sun sets over it.

Robbie Mortimer recalled that when he was a boy he saw five coaches rolling up the brae with people going to see the circle. That sort of thing died out in time, but interest in the stones has been reawakened lately. There are, however, no charabancs; now they come in their cars. He told me about a party of Japanese who came to film the stones. They waited until it was dark and then set up their equipment. The hill became a blaze

The stone circle at Old Keig.

of light. Robbie saw it from his window. It was very effective, he said, but it was a wee bit eerie.

There is another stone circle in Keig which might be regarded as even more eerie. It is on Cothiemuir Hill, near My Lord's Throat, and its recumbent stone has hollows on its surface which are known as the Devil's Hoofmarks.

I left Keig reluctantly. I hadn't solved the mystery of Wealthytown, but I had passed through Paradise, had seen the Mither Tap with the 'win'-cairdit clouds drifting by,' and had made my obeisance to My Lord's Throat. Maybe, I thought, whoever had struck on that provocative place name had seen not money, but a wealth of contentment in the cottar houses and *touns* of a bygone age.

6

AUL' CHANNRY KNAP

Auchenten', Strathen', Stones
  an' Merrytap,
Gushetneuks and Baassies an'
  aul' Channry Knap

These lines were chanted in the bothies and barnyards of Buchan in the days when place-name rhymes were in vogue. They were farm names from the Cruden area. Auchentend was from the Gaelic *Ach an tein*, meaning 'field of fire,' but what intriguing story lay behind that I never discovered. Strathend (pronounced Strathyne) was a neighbouring farm, and both stood on the main road from Ellon to Peterhead. 'Strathies' was well known as the place where the coach horses were changed.

Stones Farm lay less than a mile to the north, at Hatton. Up until the eighteenth century stone houses were few and far between. A description of Longside parish in 1723 read: 'Upon the lands of Ludquhairn there is a pretty ston house . . . the lands of Buthla and Thunderton having no stone houses upon them.' I found Merrytap on an OS map, not far from the Stones, but there was no sign of Gushetneuk or Baassies. Some people remembered the name Gushetneuk, but couldn't pinpoint it.

I wondered if there had been a Gushetneuk at Hatton in some earlier period. One chap thought I was looking for *Johnny Gibb of Gushetneuk*. Later, I dug out William Alexander's book to read the description of *his* Gushetneuk: 'Round the corner of the wood from Gushetneuk, and a little beyond where a trotting burnie came down the hollow, there stood a small hamlet, consisting of about half a dozen unpretending edifices, scattered here and there, including the smith's and shoemaker's places of abode . . . this was Smiddyward.'

Well, there were some unpretending edifices in Hatton; there were trotting burnies running down to the Water of Cruden; and there had certainly been a souter there, more than one if I remember rightly, for when my father was a fee'd loon at Chanonry Knap (the last farm in the place rhyme) he would walk up to the souter's shop in the evening to have a dram with other farm workers. William Alexander gave only one Gushetneuk, in Oyne, but there were probably Gushetneuks all over Buchan. The name meant 'the corner of a recess or angular place'.

Baassies defeated me. The spelling was obviously wrong, and I couldn't match the sound to any name, although someone suggested Ba-hill. There was a Ba-hill at Auchnacoy. It turned out that Baassies wasn't the name of a farm, it was a man's nickname, but I never found out who he was.

At any rate, I started my search at Stones Farm. Duncan Wyness had been there for thirty years, and before that was at Bogbrae. There are a number of 'stony' farms listed in *Place-Names of Aberdeenshire*, among them Stonefolds, Stonehouse, Stonehousehill, Stonekiln and Stonemill. James Macdonald produced a few more in *Place Names of West*

George Anderson in his garden at Hatton.

Aberdeenshire, including a Stonyfield at Drumblade in Strathbogie. 'So called,' he wrote, 'from a stone circle on a field beside the farm steading'. Ten stones still remain on the ground, but many were broken up and removed above seventy years ago (early nineteenth century).

At one time, farmers thought nothing of knocking down standing stones and stone circles and using them for building work on their farms. Duncan Wyness told me there had been a stone circle at Stones Farm that was demolished. George Anderson, who farmed at Stones before Duncan took over, confessed that his grandfather had been responsible. He wanted the stones to build a steading.

Merrytap (Merrytop on OS maps) was in a field on Stones Farm, across from George's house. It was a ruin, burned down after Duncan Wyness went to Stones. Later, the roof fell in. Merrytap was one of a number of 'merry' place names. James Macdonald mentions a Merryhaugh, a Merryhillock and Happyhillock, but he couldn't come up with a convincing explanation of why they were all so happy. He said there was a Merryhaugh at Rhynie and thought there 'may have been a play ground in old times,' but it seemed a feeble explanation.

Merrytap must have been the saddest of all the merry ferm toons. It lay there, crumbling into dust, its windows gazing eyeless across the farmland. Yet at one time it had probably been 'a pretty ston house' like the one at

All that remains of Merrytap, where Babbie Mungo is said to have lived.

Ludquhairn. From the walls and windows I could make out that there had been two houses, close to each other. I had been told that sixty or seventy years ago an old lady called Babbie Mungi lived there. She had no land, just a house, but she kept hens and was always seen going up to the local shop to sell her eggs.

George Anderson told me there had been two cottar houses there, used to house farm workers from the farm. Two of his men had lived there for a long time, a second horseman and a cattleman. George remembered Babbie Mungo. She had lived at a place near Connon's Croft, but her house had no name – it was simply called Babbie's house. I discovered later that Babbie *had* lived at Merrytap, but it was long before George's time there.

So that was the end of the ill-named Merrytap and Babbie's tale. I left Hatton and headed south to Cruden and Chanonry Knap. I was to run into more problems there. Chanonry Knap was originally in the Ordnance Survey map, but for some reason or other was taken out of it. I thought it must have been demolished, but when I checked a map much later I saw a farm called Kirkton where Chanonry Knapp had been.

When I drove there from Hatton it was shut up, there was nobody there, so I asked a neighbour its name.

'Kirkton,' she said.

'So where's Chanonry Knap?' I asked.

'That's it!'

It seemed that Chanonry Knap had been renamed. The old names tell you something about the ferm touns and the people who lived in them, so why anyone should change it to 'Kirkton' was beyond my understanding. Later, when I met the present owner, Dominique Brunning, she said it was still Chanonry Knap, or, more specifically, 'Chanonry Knap and Kirkton'. That was how it was described in a solicitor's letter she got during the purchase of the farm. But the question still nagged me – which came first, Chanonry Knap or Kirkton. Dominique bought the farm in 1989. She keeps Shetland ponies, eight of them when I was there, two more on the way. She told me that in 1894 a minister had bought the farm. This may have had some influence on the name, although 'Chanonry' had a kirk connotation. 'Knap' means a knoll.

There was one more farm in that place rhyme that I was told I should see – Auchenten. There was a 'For Sale' sign at the road-end when I arrived. The sun sparkled on a mill pond and daffodils threw a bright splash of colour over the scene, but they did little to blunt the shock I felt

The farmhouse at Chanonry Knap, where the author's father was
born and brought up.

at the utter desolation all around me. This was more than a 'field of fire'; it
seemed as if a demolition squad had swept through it. The house and farm
buildings were in ruins, slates peeled from the rooftops, doors lurched to
the ground, windows had gone. Through one window in the farmhouse I
could see a fridge. I thought of the days when the smell of oatcakes, made
on a griddle, would have come drifting out of that kitchen. Debris lay all
about the farm.

The track ran past the farm buildings and curved away to nowhere. The
map showed a footpath at the end of it and there were other farms with
paths running into what I imagine had been a peat moss. Near Auchenten
three cottar houses stood on the edge of the track. They were all empty,
doors open, rooms abandoned. I had come to Auchenten because I was
told it had been an attractive farm and there was little doubt that this was
so, for it stood in a pretty wooded setting, but the death knell had sounded
for Auchenten, as it had for Merrytap.

Back on the road to Hatton I was looking across the flat Buchan
landscape to where there was a croft called Auchleuchries – *Ach luachrach*,
'field of rushes'. This was where John Murdoch, my grandfather on my
mother's side, saw out his days, looked after by a housekeeper called

The deserted farmhouse at Auchenten, once an attractive farm, now in ruins.

Bathie, whom he later married. I still remember the stone-slabbed floor and the big open fire with pots bubbling on the swey. There was a porch with hens clucking about the doorway, and inside the house was a big box-bed with doors that shut Grandfather Murdoch away from the outside world.

Sometimes, when I was there, I would wander down the croft field to puddle about in the burn at the bottom of it and I would sit at the road end and watch the bus from Mintlaw go grumbling past on its way to Ellon. In those days I gave no thought to the crofts and farms around Auchleuchries or to their strange-sounding names; Byreleask, for instance, or Waterloo (where did *that* come from?), or Kiplaw and Mulonachie. There were a lot more . . .

Now, a lifetime later, I scrabble about among old maps and papers searching for intriguing place names, wondering what they mean, where they came from, and who turned them into verse. Place rhymes were all the rage on farm touns in the old days. Put them together and you would have a gazetteer of half the farms in Buchan, or Deeside, or wherever the ploughmen poets were at work. It used to be said that bothy ballads were made by people who couldn't write for people who couldn't read.

Meikle Wartle is a picturesque little hamlet near the Kirkton of Rayne, north of Old Rayne, where a famous cattle and horse market, the Lourin Fair, was once held. There is also a Little Wartle, not shown on the map. Both Wartles were featured in place rhymes. The first, the shorter of the two, went like this:

Muckle Wartle, Little Wartle,
Red Kirk o' Rayne,
Bonnyton an Boonie,
An' a sall be yer ain.   *all shall be your own*

The second rhyme is longer, with more names, and the Red Kirk becomes the White Kirk:

There's Easterton and Westerton
    Saphock an Pitblane
Little Wartle, Muckle Wartle,
An the Fite Kirk o Rayne,
Bonnyton an Baddyfash,
An a sall be yer ain,
An ye sall sit at Tocherford
An see the boats come hame.

I have often wondered what untold story lay behind the Muckle Wartle rhymes, with their roll-call of names and their promise that 'a sall be yer ain'. Even more intriguing is the final pledge about Tocherford. Tocherford is a farm two miles north of the Kirkton of Rayne, just off the Oldmeldrum road. It sits at the bottom of the Hill of Rothmaise, with farmlands stretching away from it as far as the eye can see. Yet this was where they would sit 'an see the boats come hame'.

There is a Tocher and an Over Tocher nearby and the Gaelic word *Tochar* means a causeway. There is a Causewayfold near Muckle Wartle. William Alexander, in his *Place-Names of Aberdeenshire,* wrote, 'In practically all cases where causeway occurs, the place is upon the line of one of the old roads at a point where a moss was crossed by a 'causeway'. For instance, where the old Banff road crossed the moss of Perwinnes at Scotstown Moor; or again, on the Old Deer to Crimond road, where there were the muckle and little causeways of Kininmonth.'

Muckle Ythsie and Little Ythsie also claim a place in place rhyme literature. Ythsie is in Buchan, its situation marked by the Prop of Ythsie, a monument erected on the Hill of Ythsie by the tenants of Haddo estate to the memory of their laird, George Gordon, 4th Earl of Aberdeen, who was Prime Minister from 1852 to 1855. They say that from the Prop you get the finest view of Buchan.

I first climbed the Prop many years ago. Up on the top, I remembered a line from one of J.C. Milne's poems, 'Oh Lord look doon on Buchan an a' its fairmer chiels.' I couldn't see the fairmer chiels, but I could see the farms, spread in front of me as far as the eye could see . . . a splatter of Ythsies, a few crofts and cairns, *three* Little Meldrums, a Boghouse (in 1613 it was called 'Ower Boighous of Tolquhone'), a Raxton and a Shethin.

Raxton and Shethin appeared in the Ythsie place rhyme. Shethin was an old farming estate. It once had a castle, demolished in 1644 on the orders of Covenant leaders. Raxton (it is spelt Braxton in the rhyme) was originally part of the lands of Shethin.

The road to Ellon runs through Ythsie-land and to the north of it is a rash of Auchedly farms; the Mill of Auchedly, Burnside of Auchedly, the Mains of Auchedly, Northseat of Auchedly, and so on. I counted eight in all. This is what the place rhyme had to say about Auchedly and the other fairmer chiels:

Muckle Ysie, Little Ysie,
Braxton and Shethin,
But the like o' these Aucheedlies
My fit wiz never in.

The Muckle Ythsie verse was short and to the point, but most of the rhymsters tried to crowd as many names as they could into their verse. The following is a typical example:

Caulkail and Monymusk,
In'rurie, the Perk and the Peel,
Drumoak and Inverneil,
Tillydaff and Tillyboy,
Back again to Drumnahoy,
Avexshiel and Nethershiel,
And Shiel Shiel's Brae,
And ower the Fork and Kaberty,
The Mill o' Corsonday,
Aberdeen and Aberdour,
Mill o' Camphol and Craigvour.

So on and on it went, place rhymes forming, as one writer put it, 'compendiums of rural geography'. But place rhymes were more than a mere record of 'borough toons' and 'ferm toons'. They were a medium of social commentary and a platform for the dry, uncompromising humour of the North-east. The place-rhyme poets honed their wit to a needle-sharp and often wickedly-wounding point. For instance, they loftily dismissed the 'middlin' or mediocre folk of Birse on Deeside with this verse:

> Easter Cleen and Wester Cleen,
> An' Percie and Dalsack,
> An' a' the bodies thereaboot,
> They are a middlin' pack.

Insults flew backwards and forwards between the towns and villages. The folk of Fraserburgh had a name for the villagers of Strichen, whose homes were close to the peat mosses. They called them 'Strichen Peats'. Back came the jibe – 'Holy Brochers'.

'The Mutton-ruggers o' Rathen' got their nickname because some of them were said to help themselves to their neighbours' sheep. Then there were the 'Tarland Tykes' and 'the Leochel Tummlers', the 'Tomintoul Shearers' and 'the Crovie Queets', 'the Heatherscrapers o' Cromar' and 'the Macduff Geets', 'the Dub-skelpers o' Auld Deer' and 'the Caul Carles of Tornahaish' . . .

Tornahaish is a hill at Corgarff. It gets its name from *Torran a' chaise*, 'little knoll of the cheese'. Alexander Laing, in his 'Donian Tourist' in 1828, said that 'many translate the hill where the fairies performed their magic round.' William Alexander thought that Laing's theory pointed to *Torran thaibhse*, from *taibhse*, an apparition. So there is the choice – cheese, fairies or ghosts!

Tomnahaish and another Corgarff hill, Carnavachtan, feature in a weather couplet:

> When there's mist on Carnavachtan
> There's drift in Tomnahaish.

Back to the names:

> The Nochty Gallopers
> The Glenbuck Boddies
> The Donside men
> The Maisie Mackers o' Pennan
> The Chow-baits o' Rosehearty
> The Moggan-hose o' Pitullie

The Aisie Tods o' Broadsea
The Hungry Hole o' the Broch
The Backbar o' Rottery
An' the Sanel Trip.

I thought Sanel might have been the local pronunciation of Sandhole. There had been an inn called 'The Sandhole' at Longside, but it turned out that this Sanel was at Cairnbulg. The Rottery, with its Backbar, defeated me. As with so many of these old rhymes, I am left wondering what it means.

Pitullie, south-east of Rosehearty, is one of the three Pits of Hell. That's what a sour-tongued minister called it when it broke away from the parish of Aberdour in 1633, along with Pittendrum and Pitsligo. When you think of Moggans (long fishers' stockings) you think of the Blue Mogganers of Peterhead, but Pitullie must have tried to out do the Blue Toon in the place-name battle. According to one source, the Aisie Tods of Broadsea were the 'airsie' tods. I gave up on the Rottery and the Sanel.

Banff and Cullen came in for a bit of stick from the rhymsters:

Banff it is a borrows toon,
A kirk withoot a steeple,
A midden o' dirt at ilky door,
A very unceevil people.

and:

Aiberdeen 'ill be a green
An Banff a borrows toon,
An Turra 'ill be a restin place,
As men walk up and doon;
Bit Cullen 'ill remain the same,
A peer fool fisher toon.

With all this vitriol flying about between villages, it seems that the womenfolk of Fochabers tried to drown their sorrow with the bottle. This is what happened:

Aw sing a sang, aw ming a mang,
A cyarlin an a kid;
The drunken wives of Fochabers
Is a' rinnin wid.

Maybe Auld Nick was behind all the trouble. There were a number of verses about the Devil being dead and buried in Kirkcaldy, but it was said that he had sprung to life again and was dancing with joy:

> Some say the deil's dead
> An beerit in Kirkcaldy,   *buried*
> Some say he's up again
> An dancin 'Heilan Laddie'.

In fact, he was neither, for yet another verse had transported him to France:

> Some say the deil's dead
> An berrit in Brest Harbour,
> Some say he's risen again
> An prenticed to a barber.

There was scarcely a village in the north-east that didn't get dragged into the place-name game. In came 'the Drainie Drabs', 'the Duffus Knabs', 'the Peas-wisps of Covesea' and 'the Burnt-shins of Alves'. Occasionally, in a weak moment, some soft-hearted rhymster would decide to say a good word about some of the towns. For instance:

> Dipple, Dundarcus,
> Dandilieth and Dalvey,
> Is the four bonniest haughs
> On the banks o' the Spey.

It took a Fraserburgh versifier to turn out what must surely have been one of the most vicious couplets written during the place-name poetry era. There was nothing to show who it was aimed at, or who actually wrote it, but this is what it said:

> Lazy, lazy, buggerin bodie,
> Bare-arsed, hirplin thing.   *crippling*

The North-east coast is a minefield of tortuous place names. Go west to the Braes of Enzie – 'a place full of wonders,' I once wrote – and you will find yourself in a splatter of 'bonny ferms' with names like Cowfurrach, Cuttlebrae, Sauchenbush, Preshome, Dallachy and Gollachy.

> There's Dallachy and Gollachy,
> Wellheads an' Allalath,

The sand road tae Clochan, an'
Whiteashe's strait wee path.

The poet J.M. Caie, who wrote that verse in his poem 'The Enzie,' said it was 'a curnie daft aul-farrant wirds tae them that doesna ken' [a few daft old-fashioned words to them that doesn't know].

Caie wasn't the sort of poet to trade offensive verses in the name game, but there were plenty more ready to have a go. From their pens came a long list of poems sniping at rival towns and villages, some very short and to the point, for instance: 'Gyang t' Padanarm an' pick dirt in the craws.' Padanarm is in *Kirriemuir* parish, one of two hamlets in a bleak area curiously named Muir of Cabbylatch. One hamlet was called Roundyhill, the other had the biblical name of Padanaram, although it was originally called Ellerton.

Thurso in the far north became a target for a longer piece:

Oh Thursa is a dirty place,	
A town without a shirra,	*sherriff*
The fisher biggins fou o' dirt,	*cottages*
The people pridefou verra.	*full of pride*

There was a poor lookout for Montrose and Dundee, according to one versifier, who may well have come from Brechin. He wrote:

Bonnie Montrose will be a moss	
When Brechin's a borough toon,	
And Forfar will be Forfar still	
When Dundee's a' dung doon.	*knocked down*

These place-name rhymes played on the age-old rivalry between towns – the Blue Toon against the Broch, Banff against Macduff, and so on. They tilted, too, at farm servants' 'betters', as in the Leochel-Cushnie grace about the tight-fisted farmer's wife. Thin brose and nae breid, Oh, God, gin she were deid!

Although place rhymes are not regarded as having great value in the business of onomastics, Ian Fraser of the Scottish Place-Name Survey suggested that they may offer insights into sociology. 'They can tell you a lot about how the people of one village looked at the people of a neighbouring village. It was very often pejorative.'

There is an affinity between the place rhyme and the practice on the west coast of referring to other places in the district by animal names.

'This sort of totemistic approach is quite common,' comments Ian. For instance, the people of Gairloch, his home town, were referred to as 'cod' because they were all cod fishermen, while Aultbea were the rat people. 'Even to this day, if you are from Gairloch and mention the word 'rat' the older generation will give you a sideways glance. They'll say, "Mmm!" One of the cods from Gairloch speaking!'

There were other curious bynames that I discovered in this part of the west coast. The folk in Inverasdale on Loch Ewe were known as 'the Cannibals', and farther up the loch at Cove were 'the Goats'. People in Badfern were 'the Hens' and at Badcall on Loch Broom there were 'the Cows'. I was told that there was once a teacher at Loch Broom who was known as 'Polly Cow'. When she came into her classroom one morning she found a sheaf of corn lying on her desk.

The villagers in Poolewe, near Aultbea, got short shrift – they were called 'the Tinkers'. It wasn't until much later that I went on holiday to Aultbea, a place I have returned to time and time again. I have never had the nerve to ask the folk there why they are called 'rats'.

7

CREESHIE RAW

They called it the Creeshie Raw. It was just a jumble of old cottages stuck against a dyke on a back road in Buchan. The first time I saw it, some seventeen years ago, it was buried under ivy and weeds. The word 'creeshie' means greasy – Greasy Row – and the cottages stood on the roadside at Invereddie, a few miles from Longside. They were occupied by women working in the carding and spinning departments of the Kilgour Woollen Mill, near the steading of Nether Kinmundy Farm.

Local youngsters taunted the 'creeshie' folk with a piece of doggerel that went:

Creeshie beagle, tatie thief,	oddly-dressed figure
Four and twenty airn teeth,	iron
Yin to ca' and yin to girn,	*drive; catch*
An' yin to ca' the creeshie pirn.	*reel*

The stone dyke on the road formed the back wall of the cottages, about nine or ten of them. One of the cottages was used as a shop and licensed premises. They were all thatched and some had wooden chimneys, which made them a great fire risk. But it was time and the weather, not fire, that put an end to the Creeshie Raw.

When Charlie Penny, the tenant farmer at Nether Kinmundy, bought the farm for about £17 an acre, he got the Creeshie Raw thrown in for nothing. He charged the Creeshie tenants about £5 a year for each cottage, adding on a bit for the one used as a shop. The shop was then run by Norman Davidson, who later became a dairy farmer at Hillhead of Gask in Cruden. Later, Tammie Beagrie and his wife took it over, helped at the counter by their red-haired daughter, Dolly.

When the woollen mill closed down, the workers made tallow candles from the fat or 'creesh' of sheep and oxen, and it was this more than anything that gave this tiny community the unkind nickname of Creeshie Raw.

Nether Kinmundy was literally a *near* neighbour to the Mains of Kinmundy. Both were large farms and it was said that no two farms in Buchan were closer to each other. When Charlie Penny retired in 1930, both farms were taken over by James Taylor, the Mains farmer.

I wrote about the Creeshie Raw in my book *Discovering Aberdeenshire* and I thought then that the verse was a piece of local doggerel. It was only recently that I discovered that the same verse was being chanted in the streets of Galashiels and Selkirk – as far back as the middle of the nineteenth century.

James Cockburn, who came from that area, wrote in *Scottish Notes and Queries* in 1869 about the time:

> When weavers went about with their aprons on, and broad Kilmarnock or Tam O'Shanter bonnets, or mayhap woollen pirnies for head gear, with moleskin or corduroy for working clothing.
>
> 'Creeshie was the name given to boys and girls who worked in the local woollen trade in the carding and spinning departments, and were either "feeders" or "piecers".' 'The piecers attended to the *Billy* and "pieced" or mended the "rowans" or rovings as they were drawn in by the slubber. When the supply of rowans got short the piecers called out: "No a rowan, stop – no a draw, stop" – until the slubber stopped the Billy, and either sat down in a corner or went out until the rowans gathered in sufficient quantity to enable him to resume work again.
>
> If he went out, which he frequently did, the opportunity would be taken of reading, or telling stories, and propounding guesses, or riddles. Sometimes also a ploy would be laid to give some one a 'Creeshie bite,' which consisted of a bit of wool dipt in oil, or tar, or worse. This was slipped or forced into the mouth of the victim, who, when goaded to anger by the jeers and laughter of the operators, would strike out, and many a bloody nose and black eye resulted from the administration of the 'Creeshie bite'.

When a young lad went to learn the weaving trade he would be told to learn the weavers' 'word', which went:

If ee wants to come good speed,	*you*
Keep eer temples near the reed;	*your*
If ee wants to mak' a wunnin,	*winning*
Keep the shuttle constant runnin'.	

Cockburn once heard an old weaver giving another piece of poetic advice to a young weaver:

If ye wab's ower hard, blaw water on't and it'll saffen't,	*web; soften*
If ye wab's ower saft, blaw water on't and it'll teuchin't.	*toughen it*

Water, apparently, was his cure for all the ills that afflicted the weaving business.

Weavers were subjected to all sorts of jeers and jibes. Boys and girls thinking about their careers were said to chant the following:

Aw wadna be a weaver be ony, O,	*by any*
Aw wadna be a weaver be ony, O,	
For he sits an' he girns, an' ca's the creeshie pirn,	
Aw wadna be a weaver be ony, O.	

Interestingly, the folk of Galashiels gave the Selkirk people rude nicknames, just like the folk of the north-east (see Chapter 6), and the Selkirk folk did the same. People in Galashiels were called 'Herons' and those in Selkirk were called 'Craws'. Galashiel boys going to Selkirk were bombarded with cries of 'Heron, Heron,' or the warning:

Heron, heron, hide eer head,
The Selkirk craws will pike ee dead.

Then there was the two-liner that went:

The Galashiels herons, lockit in a box,
Daurna show their heads for the Selkirk game cocks.

The days of the Creeshie folk are long since gone, both in Buchan and the Borders, and there are no more cries of 'Creeshie beagle, tatie thief' and no more threats that 'the craws are comin' to bury ee dead'.

8

SIX WONDERS OF BUCHAN

I call them the Six Wonders of Buchan. They have never been given any official recognition, for they were the personal selection of the Countess of Erroll, who wrote in her historical notice of Buchan:

> The things most remarkable in Buchan seem to be 1. The Parish of Forvey, which is wholly overblown with sand; 2. The Dropping Cave of Slains; 3. Bullers-Buchan near the Bownes; 4. The Well of Peterhead; 5. The multitude of *Selches* that come in at Strabegge; 6. Eagles which build in the Craigs of Pennan.

The Forvie sands and Bullers of Buchan are well known, and Strabegge, where the selches – seals – came in was the Loch of Strathbeg. The name is pronounced Strabeg. The well in the Blue Toun was the Wine Well, a celebrated mineral well, which was demolished in 1936, and the Dropping Cave of Slains was described in Dr John Pratt's *Buchan* as 'among the chief natural curiosities of the district'. He said it was remarkable for the number and beauty of its stalactites.

James Dalgarno, a writer and antiquarian, wrote about the Dropping Cave in an article in *Scottish Notes and Queries* in 1888. He called it the Dripping Cave, which was probably more accurate, and he described in detail its 'milk-white stalactites, incrusted on the rocks, ledge upon ledge from the top to the bottom, the whole plutonic scene of rugged arches and gloomy passages, goblin-like imagery, the slimy cells, and constant drippings.'

Bullars of Buchan.

The Countess of Erroll must have had a difficult task sorting out her claimants for the Six Wonders of Buchan, for along this turbulent coast is a remarkable collection of caves and rocks. There is Cove Arthur, larger than the Dropping Cave, where Dalgarno found 'slimy cells and broken-down galleries, the whole reminding us of a huge cathedral disjointed by an earthquake,' and there is the Blin' Man's Rock – how it got that name I never discovered – where smugglers had a secret vault, a receptacle for Holland gin and French brandy.

This is a land where the past sits on your shoulder like a hobgoblin, reminding you of dark and fearful happenings: of how in 1597 three women were taken to the Gallow Hill, bound to a stake, and 'brint to the deid' for using charms, witchcraft and sorcery; and of the time, in May 1836, when Tammas Robertson, a Forvie fisherman, saw and spoke with a mermaid and was told he would never meet with a watery grave. He never did.

It is a land which was once 'a wild waste of heath and boggy marshes, with here and there on a dry knoll grey stone cairns, serving as hiding places to the pole-cat, weasel and lizard; but which had been raised many ages before to mark the place where the ancients fought and fell and where the survivors had made mourning and burning for them.'

When I was following James Dalgarno's footsteps through Slains it took me to the Meikle Loch, where I once watched greylag geese come winging in under a dying sun after a day in the fields. The loch lies just off the road to Cruden, not far from a farm called Knapperna. It was on another farm, Chanonry Knap, farther up the road, that my father worked as a fee'd loon before going up to Aberdeen to join the police. There were other knaps (hillocks) in the area. North of the Meikle Loch was Knapsleask and all around it was a clutter of Leask farms: Mains of Leask, Nether Leason, Mill of Leask, Moss Leask, Milton of Leask and East Byreleask.

The House of Leask began as Leask, a Cuming property, in the early eighteenth century, but became Gordon Lodge on the marriage of Barbara Cuming to Dr Alexander Gordon of Hilton and Straloch, a descendant of the Gordons of Pitlurg in Banffshire. Their grandson, a major-general, renamed it Pitlurg after the ancestral lands. His son, Captain Gordon Cumming Skene of Pitlurg, Dyce and Parkhill, commissioned the architect Archibald Simpson to build the House of Leask in 1826–27 and returned it to the original name.

There is another Leask building that might be a candidate for the Countess of Erroll's list – the Old Chapel of Leask, the seventh wonder of Buchan. Its proper name is St Fidamnan's Chapel (St Adamnan's) and it was probably built in the 15th century. This ancient chapel sits on Knapsleask, a ruinous rectangle of stone whose three-feet thick walls have been buffeted and blasted by Buchan storms for many centuries.

Dalgarno wrote about the people who were buried within the walls of the chapel, 'their mouldering bones wasting within these narrow bounds.' He said that General Gordon of Pitlurg had preserved 'this fine old ruin' by having it walled and planted with trees.

James Dalgarno's wanderings took him down to the Chapel of Leask by the Ferny Brae, which lies near to the centre of the Moss of Lochlundie. From there you can see the whole boundaries of the parish of Slains. It was said to be surrounded by water at one time. 'From time immemorial,' wrote Dalgarno:

> The Ferny Brae was known only as a covert to the foxes, badgers and birds
> of prey. Some of the older parishioners to this day assert that it was haunted
> by goblin and spectres.
>
> An old man, who died in 1875, in his 93rd year used to relate how, when

Lambing time at the Meikle Loch on the A975 road near Newburgh. Here, hundreds of greylag geese can be seen winging their way in under a dying sun after a day in the fields.

about eighteen, he and his master's daughter, a little girl, went bird-nesting there one summer Sabbath morning, and when in the act of lifting a prize of moor fowl's eggs they heard an angry growl, which made the blue 'heathen' stones (gneiss) ring. The girl became alarmed, clung to him for protection, and directed his attention to what he thought was a calf. On looking round he saw a large grisly monster finding his way into an opening below a large stone. The eggs were left untouched and both went home at a much quicker pace than they left it.

In the spring of 1830, a man named William Wildgoose became tenant of Ferny Brae. He removed the large 'heathen' stones and cairns for building purposes and the ferns, foxgloves and bluebells that had grown undisturbed for hundreds of years were uprooted – and it was discovered that the 'island' had been an ancient burial ground. There were decaying human bones there.

Wildgoose found some flint arrow-heads and perforated flints and used them as charms against witchcraft by placing them over the doors of his house and byre – a common practice in those superstitious days. In November 1875 Dalgarno came into possession of a finely polished celt

The crumbling ruins of the Chapel of Leask, north of the Meikle Loch in Buchan. It was said that there were 'many spectral stories about the Chapel and its surroundings'. It stands near a cluster of Leask farms. In the fifteenth century the estate of Leask (pronounced Lesk) was broken into two parts named Gowune and Brogan. These were family names. In modern times it was style Pitlurg.

(axe) of chalcedonic flint, about 7 inches long. It was found in the house at Ferny Brae, wrapped in flannel 'as black as the sooty rafters'. In all probability, said Dalgarno, it had been concealed there as a charm for fifty years, and dated from the time that William Wildgoose had begun life as a farmer. General Gordon's servant, John Leith, had some curious stories to tell about Slains and the Chapel of Leask, but Dalgarno didn't elaborate on them. He indicated that the building of the general's wall put an end to all these spooky ongoings. 'Leith,' he wrote, 'used to relate many spectral stories about the Chapel and its surroundings, but the "shades of the departed" were forever laid at rest after the General's orders were fully carried out.' In laying out the ground John came upon a stone, partly dressed, measuring four feet long by two and a half broad, with what he said was 'an *unreadable inscription,* which may be still within the walls.' The italics were Dalgarno's, hinting that the inscription had some unpleasant message.

Less than a mile from the chapel, the OS map shows a mound called the Pole Hill. William Alexander, in his *Place-Names of Aberdeenshire*, describes it as 'an artificial mound of some size and of unknown age.' Dalgarno called it the Poll-hill of Leask. The mound, resembling a ship with the keel uppermost, measured upwards of 90 ft by 32 ft. It terminated in a point at both sides. General Gordon also had 'this curious mound' walled in. The site was his favourite haunt and he called it his 'Observatory'.

About a mile north of the Poll Hill, three farms called Bogbrae are shown on the OS map. One stands on the Ellon road, near Auchenten and Strathend, the farms mentioned in the place-name rhyme. There is a second Bogbrae half a mile away and a Little Bogbrae on a side road leading to the Chapel of Leask. It was at one of these that some very odd things happened some sixty years before James Dalgarno wrote about the Chapel of Leask.

There was a prominent mound on the farm of Bogbrae, which was known as the Elfin-knap. Dalgarno said that many weird stories were still being told about the farm in his time, but the mound was demolished when part of the farm was being reclaimed. When that happened, four stone pillars, more than 4 feet high, were found, supporting slabs of stone which acted as a roof. Was this the home of the wee folk?

Thomas Bowman, the farmer at Bogbrae, the Elfin-knap, once took James Dalgarno to the farm of Woodend, Belscamphie, and pointed out a site called 'The Guidman's Fauld', which he said was dedicated or set apart for the elfin king. In other words, a piece of the farm belonged to the Devil. The practice of leaving a plot of land uncultivated to propitiate Auld Nick was common four or five centuries ago, but the clergy came down hard on farmers who made such a pact. An extract from the sessional records of Slains in 1649 shows how the Belscamphie case was handled.

At a meeting on 18 November, the minister asked the elders if they knew any piece of land within the parish that had been called the Goodman's Land, or Fauld, or dedicated to Satan, or left to 'ly unlabourit'. They said there was a piece of land at Brogan which was called the Garlet, or Guidman's Fauld, within Andrew Robb's 'tack' (holding). The name meant it was 'a devil's acre'. It had not been cultivated for many years, but no one knew why. The minister asked them to find out why it lay 'unlabourit'.

Seven days later, the minister intimated from his pulpit that if any man within the parish knew any piece of land or parcel of ground that was called the Guidman's Land and was not being cultivated they should inform the session so that the matter might be brought before them.

On the same day, James Wilken, an elder, let the session know that Thomas Paterson, the tenant of Belscamphie, had told him that that there was 'ane piece of land in his tak calit the Guidmanes land and fauld, which was not labourit thus maney yeires.' Paterson was summoned before the session on 30 December and confessed that there was 'ane piece of land in his rowme (farm) calit the guidmanes fauld quhilk was this long time unlabourit.' Paterson was ordered to 'labour it' and promised to do so after Whitsunday.

The Devil's Acre wasn't the only thing that troubled the clergy at that time. The pagan celebrations of Yule and Halloween also came under their scrutiny and at the session's meeting in November 1649 it was intimated 'that Yuill be not keepit, but they yok yr oxin and horse and imploy yr servantis in yeir service that dayis asweel as in aney other work day.' It was also intimated that there should be no Midsummer or Halloween fires under pain of being 'punishit'.

So that was Slains, with its knaps and knolls, its bogs and mosses, its goblins and spectres. Whether or not Dalgarno believed in elves and fairies was never made clear, but he was certainly fascinated by them. He also wrote an article about elf-shots, flint arrow-heads used by elves against their enemies. He told of how, on an autumn morning in 1844, he met the son of an old smuggler on the Buchan coast. He was usually frank, but on this occasion he seemed to be down in the dumps.

'I've gotten an ill job this mornin' in the death o' a fine stirk (bullock) by elf-shot,' he said, 'an' the pity is he wasna fastent to a hairn tether (a halter made of hair) finn the weapon would a fa'en short o' him.'

'Are you sure it wasn't quarterill [a cattle disease] that your stirk died of?' said Dalgarno.

'That couldna be,' said the farmer, 'my neebor an' me opent up the beast an there was a hole through his heart.'

'What about the flint arrow? Did you find it?'

The farmer said they were never found. He knew of two instances where they fell short of doing an injury to the parties intended. The first was when his grandmother was a young lass, in Badenoch. It was the custom in her early days to herd the flocks and 'bucht' them in the glens [pen them] and make the dairy for the annual autumn market in Inverness.

His grandmother, tired out, went to rest in the 'bucht', fell asleep, and dreamed that she was in company with the 'good folk'. She was startled out of her dream and woke up to find a 'fairy dart' on the skirt of her coat.

She took it home and showed it to a Highland seer, who said that, though it had missed her, her first-born would die at birth. The prediction turned out to be correct.

The second instance involved another relative who lived in Buchan. A neighbouring guidwife had paid her a visit and, when she went to the door to leave, a fairy-dart fell between them from an unseen hand, but on this occasion there was no bad result.

'The narrator of these marvellous stories,' wrote Dalgarno, 'now long gone to his rest, had charm-stones, curing-stones in the shape of pebbles, and flint arrows, in his possession, which belonged to his grandmother. He would as soon have parted with his life as with them, and following the example of the ancients he expressed a wish during his lifetime to bury the precious relics with him.'

9

THE GEDDEL

The Geddel is a reef that runs out to sea at Peterhead. It faces an area of land known as the Geddel Braes and was well known to fishermen more than a century ago. But few people knew the meaning of the name. Writing in *Scottish Notes and Queries* in 1888, a contributor, signing himself 'Mormond,' said it was 'worse than Greek to every one in respect of its meaning.'

Mormond went on to say he had 'found the long-sought-for meaning of *Geddel* or the *Geddelbraes* of Peterhead.' It happened when he came by chance across the Celtic word *Geddheil,* which meant a commonty attached to a village where cows were put out to grass. It struck him then that the Geddel Braes had been used as a grazing place for the town's cows 'from beyond local memory'.

> Some fifty years ago, the town had its town-herd, but that occupation or office ceased to be. The older inhabitants easily remember the time when the herd-boys passed through the town blowing the cow-horn and in this way giving intimation to the cowkeepers to put out their cows and stirks. The herds were paid by the owners of the stock, a small sum being given for each animal cared for. The rocks or reefs running out from the land at the Geddelbraes is known to fishermen as the Giddels.

With the Geddel mystery solved, 'Mormond' went on to look at other coastal landmarks at Peterhead: the Cat-Stane, a large boulder lying at Roanheads, Baubygown, a corruption of Balnagowan, Cragnabo, the cow's rock, and the Garron. He said that some required explanation: Dundonie, Dunbeith, Collielaw, Collieburn, Cairntroddlie and the Stanyhillock.

The Buchan coast is studded with rocks and reefs and inlets. William Alexander listed more than three hundred coast-names in his *Place-Names of Aberdeenshire*, and it was by no means a complete list. It would take a patient researcher to track down the meaning of all these names, not to mention those that slipped through Alexander's net. We are left to ponder on strange-sounding names much as Pitheuchie, Hole an' Dirkie, the Cave of Bumahoy and the Quyngin, which is shown on OS maps as Quayman. There is hidden history here, for virtually every name has a story to it, but it is like trying to unravel a spider's web.

Alexander also included the names of some of the coastal villages. I had come across many of them in my travels, Burnhaven, for instance, or 'Burnie,' as the fisher poet Peter Buchan called it. His father was born and brought up there. It used to be said that 'Burnie' folk liked to tell tall tales. Peter wrote about their 'binders' (lies) in one of his poems:

> It seems to the truth ye're a stranger,
> I'm gaun by the binders ye tell,
> But it's a' richt wi'me,
> Tho'ye come wi' a lee,
> For I'm mair than half-Burnie masel'.

I once went with Peter on a nostalgic tour of his old haunts, to Roanheads and the Queenie, and down the Ware Road to Buchhaven, where farmers came with their carts to collect *ware* (seaweed) to fertilise their fields. We looked over the sea wall at Almanythie, whose natural harbour sheltered fishing boats as long ago as the eighteenth century. The name's derivation is meant auld man's hythe [harbour], and here the old salts gazed out to sea and dreamed their dreams of yesterday. On that walk with Peter I was seeing the old Peterhead, looking back to a time when there were twenty seatowns like Burnhaven in that corner of Buchan. They were strung like a necklace along the great knuckle of land that stretches from Fraserburgh to Newburgh, and you could double the figure if you extended the line to Buckie.

These fishing settlements were recorded as far back as the sixteenth century, but most had their origin in the eighteenth and nineteenth centuries. It was in 1721 that Alexander Hepburn, author of *A Description of the Countries of Buchan*, wrote this about Buchan fish and fisher touns:

It's to be observed that every parish on the Buthquahan coast hath one fisher toun at least, and many of them have two. The seas abound with fishes, such as killing, leing, codish, small and great, turbet, scate, mackrell, haddocks, whittings, flooks, sea-dogs and sea-cans, herrings, scaths, podlers gaudness, lobsters, partens, and several others. There are here, along the sea-coast, a great, many sea-calves. There is no so fishing round the island as we have in our Buthquhan coast.

So much for the fish and fisher touns of nearly three centuries ago. I am a lover of fish-food and when I hear of boats being laid up and quotas driving fishers out of jobs I look at the list above and wonder if I could settle for a poke of podlers and sea dogs or a plateful of flooks and scaths. How times change. As for the old seatowns, most of them are in ruins, or have vanished, with only a handful blossoming into ports like Fraserburgh and Peterhead.

Other things have also changed. Names have done so for a variety of reasons, and very often the local tongue has something to do with it. Take Mr Hepburn's flooks. They were probably swimming happily around the Fluke Peel near Rosehearty when the fishers of 'Buthquhan' nicked them out of the sea. Not many people would know nowadays about Fluke Peels, but a fluke is a fish – a flounder – and a 'peel' is a pool. Then there is the Inzie Head, pronounced Ingie Heid, as well as Codlin Head, Blockie Head, Murdo Head and Furrah Head, north of Boddam. Jeffrey's Map in 1739 showed it as a 'Rocky Point called Mackhurry,' but there is nothing to show who Mack was.

Coastal names that were familiar on OS maps had different names in their own communities. Even the famous Rattray Head had a different name; it was called Rottra Head. There is a stone in the old kirkyard at Crimond which carries the name of a William Seller, who was 'sometime feuar in Ratra'.

Roanheads, which was said to be the original 'Fischertoun' of Peterhead, but was swallowed up by it, is pronounced The Rinheeds, but if you go back to 1608 it was the ronheidis – and in 1795 the Ranheads. Cairnbulg, up the coast, is called Cyarnbulg by the landward folk and Cyarnbilg by the fishermen. Other villages call the Cairnbulg fishermen 'the Bilgers' or 'Bulgers'.

Before the Loch of Strathbeg existed – it was formed by drifting sands – the estuary of the Burn of Rattray connected to the sea near the farm of Old Rattray. Two castles guarded the harbour there: the Castle of Rattray at the entrance to the harbour and the Castle of Lonmay on the links at the northern end of the estuary. A settlement that grew up near the harbour was called Starnakeppie.

The settlement has gone, but at the north end of the loch is a farm called Starnafin. William Alexander thought that the first part of the word came from *stairean,* stepping stones, and that Starnakeppie probably contained the same word. Starnafin is now a visitor centre for the RSPB's reserve at the Loch of Strathbeg. When I was there, a notice board carried the information that there were 52,000 pinkfeet geese roosting on the loch, along with a large number of greylag and barnacle gees, pochards, whooper swans, teal, mallard, shovellers and others.

In his appendix of coast names, Alexander says he drew up the list to provide additions such as Sterrytan and the Manaarna Howp to the main section of the book. Sterrytan sounds as if it might also have a connection with the *stairean* entries, but I was unable to track it down. The mysterious Manaarna Howp, however, was at Cruden. This was the fishermen's name for an inlet between Dunbuy and a double arch called the Twa Een. According to Alexander, howp is the Buchan sound of 'hope', a sea inlet. As for Manaarna, our place-name expert thought it might be the name of a person mentioned by the historian Boece: Mernancus or Marnanchus, thane of Buchan.

Up in the Cabrach I once came across an old thatched cottage that had been transformed into a modern building with white painted walls. It was called Reekimlane. During the 'seven ill years' in the Cabrach, people were forced to leave their homes and eventually only one house remained occupied – and only one lum was reekin [one chimney was smoking]. It wasn't until I was chasing place names in Buchan that I came across another reekin' lum'. It was said that when St Combs was founded in 1785 there had been a lone house on top of a hill on what had been the north side of the new village. It was called Rick-its-Leen – it had a lum reekin' on its own. There have been different views on the actual site of Rick-its-Leen, but the Ordnance Survey's 6-inch map of St Combs in 1869 showed a small house that might have been the first house in St Combs.

Looming out of Alexander's list is a name that would at one time have sent a shiver down people's spines, and can still do so today. This was the Bullers, that 'monstrous cauldron', as James Boswell called it. To the south of the Bullers is Dunbuy, a yellow rock which, according to Dr Johnson, obtained 'additional celebrity' because it was mentioned in the *Antiquary.* This literary link lost some of its gloss when the doctor let it slip that it was really mostly known for its pong. 'It has its name and its colour from the dung of innumerable sea-fowls,' he said.

The sea-fowls were probably kittywakes, for beside the Bullers is Pitwartlachie, which in 1792 was described as 'The Bow of Pitwartlachie, a grand arch to which the kitty-weaks resort.' They are still making their mark on Dunbuy two centuries later.

To the south, off Whinnyfold – Finnyfa' – are the Scaurs or Skares of Cruden, a dangerous reef which gobbled up stricken ships like a shark swallowing minnows. Alexander said the Skares comprised the Mackies, including the Muckle Mackie and the farthest out, the Roan. I remember old John Cay, the last fisherman to launch his boat, the *Ebenezer,* from the beach at Whinnyfold, telling me about the rescue of the crew of the Danish steamer *Xenia* when it struck the Skares in 1903. There was a poem about it, one verse of which went:

> Whilst on the Scaurs the breakers roar,
> They rowed them all, but two, ashore,
> Such valiant deeds they've done an' more
> At Finnyfaul.

Farther south at Collieston is St Catherine's Dub, which appears in Alexander's list. The word *dub* means a pool. In this case it applies to a small sea inlet and it is said that a ship of the Spanish Armada was wrecked there in 1588. There is, however, another version of the story that says it was a Flemish ship sent from the Spanish Netherlands with arms and munitions to aid the rising of the Catholic earls of Erroll and Huntly in 1594. Alexander gave the name of the ship as the Santa Catalina and I have never forgotten it, for during the war I flew in Catalina flying boats.

Between Buchan Ness and the Donmouth, Alexander found a host of names that made your imagination work overtime – the Thief's Loup (what was the story behind that?), the Cats Bank, the Lang Busk and the Mid Busk, the Pricker, the Long Haven (there is a clutter of Havens in this part of the coast) and the Bleedy Hole.'

Cloven Stone, known back in 1559 as the Clowin Stane, is a cleft stone at the top of the cliffs near Longhaven. It was here that the march between the lands of the Hays of Erroll and Keiths of Inverugiue reached the sea. It now marks the parish boundary between Cruden and Peterhead.

Poring over these odd names, the questions come at you as if fired by Jeremy Paxman in 'University Challenge'. Who was Jamie Tam and what were the Mony Gutters? Was there really a Blinman at Old Castle and a

The Don Moo.

The Bridge of Don.

witch at Carlin Cove? Did the Nobs fancy themselves too much (or were they just rocks in the sea), and what made the Peer Man so poor? The Black Dog hovered about the tail-end of the list. This 'dog' was a well-known rock on the sands at Belhelvie and there was an intriguing story to it. It had a directional meaning – 'the win' fae the Blackdog' indicated the approach of a south-easterly gale with rain, and when that happened they said you could hear the growling of the Black Dog.

I liked the last entry in Alexander's list of coastal names. It was the Donmouth, but it was never known by that name. The folk in Aberdeen just called it the Don Moo.

10

LAND OF PEAT

Buchan – a land o' plenty,
Peat-bogs and puddock steels,   *toadstools*
Weet and clorty widder,   *bad weather*
And contermashious deils!   *contrary*

J.C. Milne

They call it the land of plenty, but it might well have been better named the land of peat, a bare, bleak place with 'nae a tree or a burn or a buss tae hap ye fae the winter's shocks.' Back in the eighteenth century, John Milne's 'contermashious' deils would have had good cause to be crotchety, for the Buchan countryside was mostly all moss and moor – 'full of boggis and mareshes', according to one report.

Almost the whole of the Inverallochy estate in the parish of Lonmay was moss, while the Loch of Inverallochy (now long gone) covered about three acres of the remainder. There was an extensive moss beside the Loch of Strathbeg and the minister of Lonmay had to get his peats from there because the Lonmay moss was exhausted. In 1752, he got them from Belfatton on the Crimonmogate estate. In 1776 there were 396 acres in Belfatton.

It was around that time that the miracle of Buchan began to unfold, a vast land reclamation scheme that was to change the face of the land. While the lairds were vying with each other to build 'new towns', crofters and small tenant farmers were levelling the ground, draining the mosses, digging ditches and building drystone dykes, stone houses, barns and stables.

Flora Garry summed it up neatly in one of her poems:

It wis jist a skelp o' the muckle furth,	*large skie; land outside*
A sklyter o' roch grun,	*rought*
Fan granfader's fader bruke it in,	
Fae the hedder an' the funn.	
Granfader sklatit barn and byre,	*painted*
Brocht water to the closs,	*close*
Pat fail-dykes ben the bare brae face,	*turf dykes*
An' a cairt road to the moss.	

Peat, however, remained a significant factor in the life of the Buchan communities. There were still the cart roads to the mosses and the smell of peat hung heavily over new and old towns. James Milne, writing about New Pitsligo in the eigteenth century, said that peat smoke was like a cloud over the village. It permeated every nook and cranny of the houses, and the villagers carried it about with them in their reek-drenched clothing.

Dr John Pratt upset New Byth folk by saying that the village was 'in the vicinity of a bleak moss-bog.' But he was right. The village was sited on a high ridge of land on a watershed formed by the east-flowing waters of the North Ugie, which, said Pratt, 'takes its rise among moors and mosses and creeping through bogs and swamps.'

It was on the fringe of this vast peatland that four of Buchan's 'new towns' were born in the eighteenth and early nineteenth century: Cuminestown (1763), New Byth (1764), New Pitsligo (1787), and New Deer (1803).

Dr Pratt was gathering material for his classic book, *Buchan*, when the last of the new settlements were finding their feet. He wrote about the Bog of Ardallie, 'not long ago an impassable morass,' now drained and cultivated, losing its former 'dark, sterile character'. He wrote about travelling along the Strichen road and seeing 'an immense peat-bog, stretching for miles into the country,' about the swamps of Croilaw and Bogenjohn, and about Mormond Hill covered with heath and peat-bogs.

Pratt saw the White Horse of Mormond on the hill, cut out in the turf, occupying a space of nearly half an acre – 'a very fine object', wrote the

The main street of Strichen stretches away to the Hill of Mormond and its famous White Horse. It was said that when land reclamation was changing the face of Buchan, gangs of men marched up the side of Mormond Hill, 'so greedy did they become for land.'

doctor. But it wasn't the white horse that drew people to the hill in those days – it was land.

'The whole world changed,' wrote Christian Watt, 'not suddenly like lightning. Gangs of men came to reclaim the land, ploughing bogs and stanks. Suddenly, huge big packs were marching up the side of Mormond Hill, so greedy did they become for land.'

When I wrote *Buchan, Land of Plenty* in 1996, I said that Dr Pratt had led me to write the book. 'John Pratt showed me the way,' I wrote, 'and I took it . . .' I dogged his footsteps when he travelled along the 'high road' from Peterhead to Banff. When they were building this road the money ran out and the road suddenly stopped at Auchnagorth, two miles north of New Byth. It became temporarily a road to nowhere and superstitious folk came to look on the area beyond it as 'an eerie, uncanny place'.

There are three Auchnagorths and two Auchnamoons, Upper and Lower. Auchnagorth, *Ach nan coirthe,* means 'the field of the standing stones' and Auchnamoon, *Ach na moine,* is 'the field of the peat moss'. They are still there, which may have added to the uneasy feeling that here you were in another world. In many ways that would have been true, for the wild countryside north of Auchnagorth sets itself apart from the rest of Buchan.

While Dr Pratt headed west to Banff, I made my way into what seemed to be an endless expanse of moorland, a world of rutted, muddy farm tracks and 'roch' cluttered farmyards, a landscape peppered with crofts and the ruins of crofts. I was heading up past the Hill of Cook, looking for the Crofts of Clochforbie, where the Earl of Fife once gave land to crofters evicted in the Highland Clearances. There were a hundred crofts at one time, but most of them have vanished. There were five small crofts on Upper Clochforbie, but they eventually went 'back to the heather'. It was in this land of peat that I found Peggy Clerk, a tiny woman, a wee wifukie, plump, rosy-cheeked, who worked her own croft at the Shalloch, east of Crudie. She was seventy-four, fiercely independent, living in a 'but and ben' where two black pots rested on the fire and a big, black kettle hung on a swey. Peats glowed and spluttered in the fireplace. 'It's afa reekie,' said Peggy. People still cut their peats on the old mosses, but now they have to pay for it.

There had been a road to the Fisherie moss from her croft, but it had fallen into disuse and she had ploughed it up. When I left Peggy I found my way to the Moss of Fisherie, where a wide stony track ran through the moorland as far as the eye could see. In this never-never land Peggy was only one of a number of wonderful characters I met or heard about. I had hoped to meet one of her fellow crofters, Babbie Stewart, who worked a 20-acre croft single-handed and had three cows and 'six little beasties'. Sadly, she died two weeks before I arrived there. She had fallen ill and had refused to leave her home because of her beasties.

I had come a century too late to meet Francis Jamieson, better known as Fruncie Marquis – he got the Marquis tag because he looked like the Marquis of Huntly. Fruncie was a colourful character who was not only an athlete but also a talented musician – 'a master with the cello, an angel with the fiddle, and a devil with the oxter pipes,' I wrote in *Buchan, Land of Plenty*. He died in September, 1903.

Fruncie had a sister, Jean, who lived with him on the Hill of Cook. She was a bit of a character herself. When the peat carts passed their door on their way back from the Moss of Fisherie she would dance about the field half-naked and, bending over, hold up her rump as a target for peat-throwers. It was said that Fruncie and Jean always had a good supply of peats.

My wanderings in this corner of Buchan ended on the Hill of Bracklamore, a large, flat hill whose name is said to come from *breaclach*, a

Bedlam in Buchan! Between Methlick and New Deer there are a number of farms named Bedlam – the Knap of Bedlam (a knap is a lumpy little hill), Hardbedlam (hard means high), North Bedlam and a dairy farm called the Myre of Bedlam. The name Myre is a reminder that this is boggy country – the Land of Peat. The old names for Bedlam were Bethleama (1687) and Baidlem (1764). There is a Mill of Auchriddie near New Deer, known at one time as the Bedlam of Auchriddie, sometimes as Old Bedlam.

spotted place. What that meant I never discovered, but it was shown on old maps as 'empty land.' That's what it was, a great, sprawling landscape that seemed to reach out to the rim of the world. The wind was whipping over its vast emptiness when I made my way back to civilisation, back to the good Doctor Pratt.

When I began my Pratt's tour of Buchan it was at the Loch of Strathbeg. Lady Anne Drummond, Countess of Erroll, said that one of the most remarkable things in the district was 'the multitude of selches (seals) that come in at Strabegge.' I wasn't greatly drawn to the countess's selches; I was more interested in the words of a Lonmay minister, the Rev. J. Forrest, who gave a talk on Lonmay place names to the Buchan Field Club. In the parish, he said, 'there were moors and mosses, and marshes abounded.'

Mosstown and Mosscroft were beside the Loch of Strathbeg, and as you move inland, across land that was once all moss and marsh, the names keep popping up on maps. There are three Mosstowns between Strathbeg and Inverallochy, and a farm called Wetness. William Alexander gave the origin of the latter name as the Old Scots *ness*, a wet place, which seemed a bit superfluous.

Down on the edge of the St Fergus Moss there is a Rottenhill. According to Alexander, in the dialect 'rotten' means a rat, but in place names 'it sometimes represents road-town.' Vying with it for the worst name in the area was Swineden.

Mr Forrest said that there were about ninety-four 'places' existing in the parish of Lonmay at the beginning of the twentieth century. He named a few that had disappeared, including The Deep, the Auld Place, and Greeneye. Greeneye is given in Alexander's collection as Greenee, with the explanation that 'an eye, Scot. *ee*, means a spring.' Place names can be confusing, but this seemed worse than most – Jamieson's Dictionary pointed out the Aberdeen definition of 'Ae ee' as one eye.

When I turned both *my* eyes on the place name Deep, I found that it was a place beside the Loch of Strathbeg. It appeared on Gordon's map, but no explanation of the name was given. Jamieson, coming to the rescue again, said that it meant the deepest part of a river. The Auld Place wasn't a broken-down cottar's house. It was the name given to the residences of the old lairds. The Castle of Lonmay was once known as the Auld Place.

Wardend was a name that Mr Forrest said 'was long a puzzle to me.' The difficulty, he said, was to know what 'ward' meant.

> It seems that in ancient times, near most farms and every laird's place, there was an enclosed field, and into this park the cattle were driven for safe keeping when there was no herd available, or for rest at night. Up to about 1745 there were no fences. Cattle wandered at their sweet will except for wards or herds. Round about the lairds' possessions alone were fences first erected to keep off the tenants' cattle.

The Rev. Mr Forrest was fairly exhaustive in his research into Lonmay place names, but some of his theories were suspect. If he wasn't certain, he took a crack at it anyway. The farmhouse of Lumbs was 'difficult.' He thought it might mean the 'clay' farm, 'lam' or 'lom' in Old English meaning clay. There was a bed of clay on the farm, which had been used for tile-making. It turned out that the most ancient name of the place was Cairnelrick, which meant 'the place of merriment'. Maybe they were laughing at the idea of changing it to Lumbs. William Alexander was stumped by the whole thing. He finally gave it up and plumped for the Scots word lums – chimneys.

When my wanderings in Lonmay had come to an end, I went back to the experts to find out what the name itself meant. Mr Forrest believed that it 'most likely meant the marsh plain,' while William Walker thought 'it looks very like Gael, *maigh*, from *magh*, a plain, level country,' with the first syllable, *lon*, meaning a bog. It seemed at one time as if the whole countryside had once been a marsh plain – a land of 'peat-bogs and puddock steels'. But the contermashious folk living in this blustery elbow of land in the North-east of Scotland would never allow that. Instead, they dug a new Buchan out of the bogs and marshes – a land of plenty.

A narrow back road near Methlick pushes its way through
peaty country to a farm with the intriguing name of Balquhindachy.
The original spelling in 1526 was Bawquhenyeicht and the name is
said to be connected with *Coinneach*, 'moss' – a Foggie-town.

11

OLD GRODDIE

Is this far they had their whisky still,   *where*
The hardy Petterson men,
Here at the fit o Morven Hill
Up abeen the 'Runny-ben'?   *above*

The smell of *usequeba* comes floating down from the dark corners of Morven. There were more stills on the hill than anyone could imagine. Over on the Cromar side there was once a building for brewing called the Brew House, with a burn running through it, and hidden in the Lary Burn was Gillanders' Still. The Gillanders had their farm there from 1809 to 1949 and by all accounts the Still has never been moved.

There was a fair-sized settlement at Lary at one time. No doubt the Lary folk benefited from the Gillanders' Still – a reward, perhaps, for keeping an eye open for the gaugers. On the other hand, not everyone thought that the Gillanders' brew was nectar. There is a Gaelic poem from Glen Gairn called 'Gillanders' Quaich', which casts doubt on it:

I've often drunk whisky
    In a bothy on the hill,
But nothing half so terrible
    As Gillanders can distil.

The 1696 Poll Book shows nine tenants at 'Larie', eight with wives. Two had sons and there was also a 'cotter', who had a wife. Later, the population increased to eighteen families. The ruins of their homes lie on the edge of the road to Morven Lodge and all the way down the brae from the farm to Laggan.

The 'Runny-ben' in the 'Pettersen' verse was the local name for Ruighe na Beinne, the cattle-run of the hill. Two fields west of Logie-Coldstone had this name and they were distinguished from each other by being called the Balhennie Ruighe na Beinne and the Groddie Ruighe na Beinne.

The verse is from a poem, 'The Groddie Still', by Elizabeth Allan, who was co-author, with Adam Watson of *The Place Names of Upper Deeside*. It is a poem that hovers between fact and fiction. Betty Allan was related to 'the hardy Pettersen men' – her great-grandmother was an Elizabeth Paterson, whose father had a farm at Groddie.

Whether or not her relatives took part in illicit whisky-making has never been very clear, although Betty remembered hearing older people speaking about the days of illicit stills. This corner of Cromar had its share of them. The poem, plucked from imagination, not from real life, first appeared in an issue of the *Deeside Field* which I edited. It was accompanied by an article called 'Yesterday's Dream', which was about an uncle of Betty's who had too great a fondness for the golden brew.

I first found Groddie when I was looking for a new way up Morven. It lay on the fringe of the hill, across the Groddie Burn and beyond Balhennie. Between Balhennie and the Morven summit was the Girnel o Groddie, a sheltered corrie where sheep were driven in a snowstorm. This seems to have been a spot on the map marked Little Cairn.

The Lands of Groddis, as they were called in 1600, were nothing to write home about. Parish registers called them Old Groddie, which seemed more appropriate. The name is said to come from *grodaidh*, a rotten place, stagnant marsh or bog. I found out how accurate this was when I began my climb up through the heather to Morven. I soon discovered I was walking on bogland. When I was well up the hill I came to a kind of sodden plateau which was full of rushes. I made my way round it and went up the last lap to the top.

It is fifteen years since I first saw Groddie Farm. Gordon Watt was the tenant farmer then. He and his wife Betty had come from Culsalmond to Logie-Coldstone and had been there for twelve years. Gordon was making plans to leave the farm, for his crops had been ravaged by rabbits. Not only that, they were churning up his woodwork; he showed me part of a door that had been gnawed away. He had come to the conclusion that it was time to get out.

I remember how we spoke about the whisky-smugglers and the stills and the detested gaugers. They had heard stories of illicit whisky-making at the back of the farm and Gordon had his own theory as to the whereabouts of the Groddie Still. Up the hill from the farm, behind a strip of woodland, there was a deer dyke, almost 6 feet high, stretching across the moor to Morven.

The dyke, which was a magnificent example of the old stone-dyker's craft, had a coping to prevent deer from getting over it. Huge stones had been taken from the hill to build it. They were dragged across the moor on what was known as a Puddock Sledge. A sheep pen formed part of the deer dyke and beside it a burn gurgled down past the farm.

Gordon thought that this was the site of the Groddie Still. From here, before afforestation took place, the whisky-makers would have had a clear view down over the Braes of Cromar. They would have seen the gaugers coming from a long way off. I was thinking of the lines from Betty Allan's poem:

Did they bile their mulch o maut, wi' bere	*boil; mault*
Grown on the Groddie grun,	*ground*
Beside the burnie runnin clear	
On the summer cattle-run?	
Did the copper kettle hide in here,	
Safe in the neuk o the wa',	*corner*
Abeen the smoory peat-fire's reek	*smothering*
Wi the worm dreep-dreepin awa?	
Did the Pettersons cairry their whisky pigs	*jars*
By the Roar tae Tullich on Dee,	
And ower the Mounth did it find its wey	
By smuggler's roads tae the sea?	
Fit like had it tasted, the Groddie dew,	*what like*
At nicht by the ingle neuk?	
Maybe some ramsh for me or you –	*strong*
A dram for hardy fowk.	

That, then, was rotten Groddie's story, but there is still Betty Allan's story of 'Yesterday's Dream' to tell. This was about Betty's great-grandfather, Charles Strachan. 'Charlie always got a bad name in our family,' wrote

Betty, 'and it's time to set the record straight.' Born in 1838 on the farm of Tulloch outside Lumphanan, he was also a bit of a poet. He married Elizabeth Paterson, daughter of Lewis Paterson, the farmer at Groddie, and eventually went off to Northumberland to become overseer on a private estate.

'Soon, however, things went drastically wrong,' wrote Betty. 'Charlie was sacked, and the young couple arrived back at Groddie, Elizabeth already pregnant with their only child, my grandmother, Jeannie.' In 1876, Charlie decided to try his luck in Australia. He would send for his wife and child in due course. The trouble was that Charlie had a problem – booze. He was seen as a 'drink-sodden charmer, handsome, personable, gifted, a singer of songs and writer of verse, but hopelessly addicted to the bottle.'

Little Jeannie was only three years old when her father left Groddie. In 1886 he was writing a homesick letter to Jeannie on her thirteenth birthday. In it he reminisced about 'dear Groddie' and the people there, especially the Paterson uncles who had taken his place in the child's life.

There was a passage in the poem which showed that 'dear Groddie' was never perfect. Back in those far-off days they were plagued with rabbits in the same way that Gordon Watt was pestered a century later, but in the old days they weren't allowed to take pot shots at bunnies. Charlie wrote about Uncle Lewie roving with his dog and his gune. He went on:

Just ask him if still he indulges or dares
To take a sly shot at the rabbits and hares;
If the law be as strict as it was long ago,
When the keepers would watch night and day
   for your Da;
When the poor farmers' crops would be eat
   to the root,
Yet these vermin preserved for the gentry
   to shoot.

Charlie said there was plenty of work for Lewie in Australia, where rabbits 'are thick as the spots in the sun'. As Betty Allan wrote in her article, it was an interesting comment at first hand on the unpopular restrictive Scottish game laws of the time, and the absence of such laws in Australia.

Betty's great-grandfather died in a mental hospital in Sydney in May, 1922, aged 84 years. Her great-grandmother Elizabeth pre-deceased him by twenty-one years, dying in 1903 aged 63. 'By that time,' wrote Betty, 'young Jeannie had a son – my father. Charlie never saw his daughter again, nor his grandson, nor the great-granddaughter who was born in his lifetime. I wonder if he even knew of her birth.'

The prodigal son never returned, but he was always troubled by the fact that he would never see his daughter – his 'wee little darling.' This is what he wrote in his poem:

> Yet I sometimes regret I can ne'er again see
> That wee little darling so cherished by me,
> For the lassie I left is a big girl grown,
> And the image engraved on my memory, gone.
> Ten years, when in childhood, a long time
>   must seem –
> To me it is just like a yesterday dream.

I left Groddie to its dreams. I was heading for Roar Hill – 'by the Roar tae Tullich on Dee' – and I was looking for a group of names that made up a place-name rhyme I had heard. They were tongue-twisting names written years ago by some anonymous scribbler and I wondered if I would be able to track down any of them. This is how the rhyme went:

> From Faandhy to Tamgleddie,
> Frae Paddockpool to Allalogie,
> There never dwelt an honest bodie.

I had just one clue – Allalogie. I remembered passing a place called Allalogie when going up Morven from Logie-Coldstone. This was by a track that peeled off the Dinnet-Logie-Coldstone road and went west by Raebush and Redburn. It led to a wide, stony track that pushed up Roar Hill, or 'the Roar' as it was often called, and across bare moorland to the Morven Burn and Morven Lodge. The Roar was sometimes spelt 'Rore' and may have come from *Ccnoc reamhar,* a thick or gross hill, which was an apt description of it.

So much for Allalogie. There was a Tom Glady Wood near Raebush, on the road to Roar Hill. This was Tam Gleddie, a heather hillock, from *Tom glaodhich,* hillock of the shouting, although what they were shouting about is anybody's guess. Maybe they were shouting from frustration, which was what I felt when I tried to find Paddockpool and Faandhu,

There are Paddockholes and Puddockholes and even a Poddachall, but not a Paddockpool. It may be that naming a house after a puddock had become socially unacceptable, for a 'Puddock' house in Fintray was changed to Froghall and a Paddock Hole in Crimond ended up as Frogmore.

Well, I am still looking for Paddockpool, but I have given up Faandhu as a bad job, although I think it may have been Feadan Dubh in lower Glen Callater. There is, at any rate, a more important problem bothering me. What was the meaning of the last line in the rhyme, which said that in that corner of Logie-Coldstone there never dwelt an honest bodie.

It may simply have been rhymsters in another district slandering Logie-Coldstone, but I kept thinking of all those stills buried in burns and bogs in Logie-Coldstone. It seemed as if the folk there were all in on the whisky-making game, despite the fact that it was illegal – in other words, from Faandhu to Tamgleddie there never dwelt an honest bodie. But it was the Groddie Still that stuck in my mind, the Groddie dew, made 'at the fit o Morven Hill, up abeen the Runny-ben.'

Over the years I often wondered if there was still a tenant at Groddie – or if the rabbits had eaten the place out of existence. Ten years had passed 'like a yesterday dream' to Charlie Strachan, and it had been longer than that since I had seen Groddie. Gordon and Betty Watt went to live in Insch when they left Logie-Coldstone and in 2003 I heard that they had both died, Betty Watt only a year earlier. I decided to go back to Groddie.

The countryside was wearing its spring coat as we drove through the woods towards Morven and when Groddie came in sight there was nothing to suggest that this was the old *grodaidh*, a rotten place, a stagnant bog. The white walls of the farmhouse gleamed in the sun and it was obvious that the rabbits hadn't eaten it away. Gavin Greenlaw, who took over Groddie twelve years ago said it was still 'moving with rabbits'. But there was nothing on the scale it had been in Gordon Watt's time.

So what had beaten the bunny menace? I knew it wasn't myxomatosis, but I asked Gavin if it was some other disease. 'Well, no,' he said, with a grin, 'I think it was a .22 bullet.' The keeper from the estate had gone to war with the rabbits and in the first year shot thousands of them.

Gavin, who is twenty-seven, has 500 acres to look after, and 170 suckler cows. If there were fieldnames on Groddie he hadn't heard of them, but a field nearby was called the Picts' Field. This was because a Pictish house was found there. It was later fenced off by the Scottish Heritage Society.

He didn't know about the hidden 'treasure' on his land – the Groddie Still. From where we stood we could see the deer dyke that Gordon Watt had mentioned, a six-foot-high wall climbing over the hill to Morven. From up there the whisky-makers could keep an eye on gaugers sniffing about down the hill.

When I was at Logie-Coldstone, Bill Clark told me of another way to

Gavin Greenlaw at Grodie Farm.

confuse the gaugers. He had heard of an illicit still that had operated at Pittentaggart, near Migvie. There, the whisky-makers had worked their still so that the smoke came spiralling innocently out of a house chimney. I had a quick look at the Groddie lum. There was no 'smoory peat-fire reek' coming out of it, so I took my leave of Gavin and headed back through the woods.

12

RED HARLAW

As I cam in by Dunidier
An'down by Netherha,
There were fifty thousand
   Hielanmen
A' marching to Harlaw.

Two miles north of Inverurie is a field shown on some old maps as the Pley Fauld. To the hundreds of motorists who pass it every day the name means nothing, yet this site is firmly rooted in Scotland's history. A fauld is a grassy area, usually a fold for cattle, and the Scots word *play* means strife, a quarrel. The 'quarrel' that broke out in this quiet corner of the Garioch was the Battle of Harlaw.

I came to Harlaw on a day when the fields were cloaked in autumn gold. To the north was Harlaw House, built in 1843 by Alexander Collie, an Aberdeen slate merchant, 'as a tribute to the memory of those brave citizens of Bon Accord who along with their noble Provost Sir Robert Davidson fell fighting for their country's rights against the usurper Donald of the Isles.' I knew Harlaw House well. When I was editor of the *Evening Express,* my managing director, Roger Ridley-Thomas, lived in that historic building.

To the south the Lochter Burn wandered away to join the Ury. It was there that the Earl of Mar and his men looked across the water to where the Highlanders waited for them. They crossed the Ury at the How Ford and converged on the ridge of Balhalgardy, the 'priest's town'. There were Maitlands farming Balhalgardy when the Battle of Harlaw was fought in 1411 – and there are still Maitlands there today.

Up on high ground in the Play Fauld is a lofty tower with the name Maitland on it – Adam Maitland, Lord Provost of Aberdeen from 1911 to 1914. He was the man behind the building of this 40-foot-high tower in memory of Provost Davidson and the burgesses who fell at Harlaw. The memorial was inaugurated on Friday 24 July 1914, the 500th anniversary of the Battle of Harlaw. The guests were taken to Harlaw on a special train that left Aberdeen from Guild Street Station – Platform No. 12 – at 2.40 p.m., arriving at precisely 3.12 p.m. They disembarked at a makeshift platform – a lorry – that was set up halfway between Inverurie and Inverramsay.

From the Harlaw tower you can look down through a fringe of trees to West Balhalgardy, a great sprawling farm where Robert ('Bertie')

The Harlaw monument, erected on the 'sair field' in 1911,
five hundred years after the event.

Maitland and his two sons, Robert and Adam, carry on the Maitland tradition. Lord Provost Adam Maitland was brother to Bertie's grandfather – his great-uncle. Bertie's wife, Jean, showed me a family tree printed out on a roll of paper that was about 20 feet long. She had traced the Balhalgardy Maitlands back to the Poll Book of 1691, but she is convinced that they were there in 1411. Alexander Keith, in *A Thousand Years of Aberdeen*, was quite clear about it. 'Adam Maitland,' he wrote, 'was a member of the family that had farmed Balhalgardy, near Inverurie, since before the battle of Harlaw.' They may even have been there long before that, for records show a Balhagerdy there in 1180.

Bertie Maitland is retired now, living in a house that looks across green fields to where Inverurie is creeping out towards them. Jean said she was glad there was a river and a railway between them. Bertie has become his own historian, with a pile of fat files about Balhalgardy and Harlaw. He told me how he had developed the farm, building new farm houses and four houses for his single men, the bothy men. He showed me relics that had come up through the Balhalgardy soil, including two crusie lamps and a horse's bridle. The metal plate that went into its mouth looked cruel and vicious.

Bertie Maitland and his wife Jean on their farm
at Balhagardy, with relics dug up from the battlefield.

Harlaw itself is like an open museum. With a map in your hand you can walk in the Pley Fauld and trace links with the blood-soaked conflict that took place nearly six centuries ago. There is the Liggar Steen, a stone which traditionally marks the camp of the Highland army. The name comes from *leaguer*, a camp. Then there is Legatesden, or Leggett's Den, as it was given in a ballad describing the fight between Forbes and 'the great Macdonell':

The first ae straik that Forbes strack,	*strike*
He garrt Macdonell reel,	*made*
An the neist ae straik that Forbes strack,	*next*
The great Macdonell fell.	
An siccan a lierachie	*such a hubbub*
I'm sure ye never saw	
As wis amo the Hielanmen	
When they saw Macdonell fa.	
An when they saw that he was deid	
They turned an ran awa,	
An they buried him in Leggett's Den,	
A large mile frae Harlaw.	

The ballad was right about Legatesden, which is 'a large mile frae Harlaw', but it was wrong about Macdonell, for it was another man that fell to Forbes' sword and was buried there.

'Siccan a lierache', says the balladeer. Such a hubbub! For me, however, the Harlaw story began at Dunnideer. I went there to follow the trail of the Heilanmen who marched into Harlaw on a July day in 1411. Dunnideer was the Hill of Gold. In 1578, in his *Historie of Scotland*, Bishop Leslie said that Dunnideer 'did abund in golde'. The sheep that ate the grass there had teeth and flesh that were yellow, 'as with the cullour of golde'. This was true enough, but in a more scientific age it was established that the deposit on their teeth was an incrustation of lime, phosphoric oxide and organic matter.

The fields around Dunnideer were yellow with 'the cullor of golde' when I climbed it, just as they were at Harlaw, but there were no sheep with yellow teeth. Up there, beside the gaunt ruin of the Castle of Dunnideer, built for Sir Joseline de Balliol in 1260, there were other things to look at, and to think about. The old Harlaw ballad had given me a clue to the route taken by the the Highlanders – 'down by Netherha' – but there was a version of it that gave another name:

This is what you see on top of Dunnideer, a ruin that has become a landmark that can be seen from miles around.

The fort on Dunnideer hill, which the Highlanders passed on their way to Harlaw.

As I cam through the Garrioch land,
And in by Over Ha,
There was sixty thousan Highland men
Marching to Harlaw.

Over Ha, or Overhall to give it its correct name, is a neighbouring farm to Netherhall in Premnay. In old Scots, the Ha' was the laird's house, but it came to mean the farmer's house, as distinguished from the cottars' house, and in some places it meant any farmhouse. The original name of both Overhall and Netherhall was the Barns. There is a Mill of Barns at the end of the Netherhall farm road.

The house and estate of Overhall formerly belonged to the Leiths, and later to the Gordons. It eventually passed to Lumsden of Auchindoir. They say that in 1922 a Captain Andrew Lumsden lost Overhall in a card game. There were twelve farms on the estate at one time.

When I looked up William Alexander's *Place-names of Aberdeenshire* it said that Overhall was formerly Overbarns and at that place in 1724 there was 'a tolerable good inn for passengers to lodge' there. This was confirmed by Bill Caldwood, the present farmer at Over Ha', who told me that there had been a coaching inn there, proof, it seemed, that here there had been a major road – the old road to Aberdeen.

Not far from the Insch railway crossing is the road to Auchleven and about a mile along it is a sign, 'Overhall,' pointing up a long, straight road to the farm. Another track from Insch comes over the Hill of Netherhall and down to the Mill of Barns. This old hill track, which is signposted, may have originally linked up with the road to Aberdeen.

The Highland host plundered Moray and then swept down through Banffshire and Strathbogie and on to Dunnideer and the Chapel of Garioch – fifty thousand men, it was said, although other balladeers increased that number to sixty thousand and up to a hundred thousand by the time they had reached Harlaw. The Chapel of Garioch was known as Logie Dirno when Donald, Lord of the Isles, brought his army to the Garioch. The name was changed in the eighteenth century, when the parish of Logie Durno was united with Fetternear. Locally, the kirktown of Chapel of Garioch was always called simply 'Chapel'.

The Mither Tap o' Bennachie looks benignly down on undulating countryside, low rounded hills and long flattish ridges. North of the Ury the eastern ridge starts at Balhaggardy on the battlefield of Harlaw and runs in a north-westerly direction by the intriguingly named Gunhill and

Overha' Farm, which lies on the route taken by the Highlanders on their way to Harlaw. Bennachie is in the background.

Leggat's Den. The name is said to be a personal one: Leggat. The ridges and hills south of the Ury run from the ruined castle of Balquhain, north-west by the mysterious Maiden Stone towards Pittodrie House and the Mither Tap.

It is at the Chapel of Garioch that you begin to hear the roar of battle. There are names all around that send out echoes of the Harlaw conflict, not least among them being Balquhain. The Leslies of Balquhain were an ambitious and aggressive race, holding a large share of territory and influence in Scotland. There was an old song about the number of Leslies at the ancestral home:

> Thick sit the Leslies on Gaudy side,
> At the back o' Bennachie.

There was one Leslie who earned himself a dubious reputation at the back o' Bennachie, retiring to a fortified eyrie on the Mither Tap to 'glower upon the Garioch till it was safe to come down.' He was Sir Andrew Leslie, the robber baron of Balquhain, who is said to have fathered seventy children, most of them illegitimate. 'In One Night,' it was reported, 'he begot Seven Children in sundry Places.' He may have contemplated

The Maiden Stone, which stands by the
roadside at 'the back o' Bennachie', a mile
from the Chapel of Garioch near Inverurie.

disappearing into his Mither Tap hideout to avoid their wrath, but he
decided on another way to appease them. 'All the Mothers lay in Child
Bed at One Time, and his (Sir Andrew's) Lady sent to every One of them
in Charity Half a Boll of Meal, Half a Boll of Malt, a Wedder, and Five
Shillings of Money' (Macfarlane's *Genealogical Collections*). It must have
seemed as if fate had given him his come-uppance at the Battle of Harlaw,
for when it was all over his six sons were among the slain.

The Castle of Balquhain today does little to boost the fame of the
Leslies. It was once a huge keep or tower; now it is a complete ruin. The
original castle was a quadrangular turreted building, with an enclosed
courtyard with towers at the front. It was burned down in a feud with the
Forbeses in 1520 and Sir William Leslie, 7th Baron of Balquhain, rebuilt it
as a high square tower or keep. It was the principal residence of the Barons
of Balquhain until 1690 when Patrick, Count Leslie, 15th Baron of
Balquhain, decided to move to Fetternear House. His son, George, and his
family continued to live there until his father's death in 1710. The Duke of

Cumberland is said to have ordered its final destruction in 1746. Only the east wall of the square tower or keep remains now.

At the roadside opposite the Balquhain ruin is a farm called Echo Vale. Mrs Ann Findlay and her husband live there. Ann has been there since she got married twenty-two years ago, her husband for the past forty-six years. She said the farm had been given the name Echo Vale because there was an echo from the castle. We went down to the roadside and I shouted across a field, 'Hello, Balquhain!' Back came the echo, 'Hello, Balquhain!' There aren't many echoes nowadays, for Ann said nobody came to see the castle. The writer Nigel Tranter must have passed this way, because he said in one of his books that Balquhain had 'a fine echo'.

I stood looking at the wall, the last remnants of Leslie pride, dismissed by one writer as 'a stern, simple square block, destitute of decoration or architectural peculiarity,' and wondered if Donald's wild Highlanders had shouted their war-cries at it and been given back a hollow echo. It was only later that I learned that it was the Earl of Mar's men who were at Balquhain, not the Highlanders. The Forbes, 'frae Curgarff to Craigievar', the Leiths, the Erskines, and the Leslies approached the battlefield by Blackhall, Drimmies Hill, and the castle of Balquhain, and there where they occupied a strong position on their own ground, to the right of the enemy.

One of the old ballads tells of a traveller who 'cam in by Dunidier, an' doun by Netherha' and met two of the defenders:

As I cam on, an farther on,
An doun by Balquhain,
Oh there I met Sir James the Rose.
Wi him Sir John the Gryme (Graham).

The vanguard of the army crossed the Ury at Mill of Keith-hall, and marched by the Fort of Caskieben and Boynds (pronounced 'Beens') to Colly Hill, where they had a commanding view of the enemy across the Lochter burn. The mounted men, led by Mar himself, crossed the Ury at Howford and on the ridge of Balhalgardy they were right in front of the Highlanders. The scene was set for Red Harlaw.

It is hard to believe that six centuries ago this peaceful countryside was made sodden with the blood of both Highlanders and Lowlanders. Little wonder that they called it 'the sair field of Harlaw.' The balladeers chronicled it in great detail, crying out the names of lairds and nobles who had fallen, among them Lord Saltoun of Rothiemay, 'a man of might and meikle main', the 'gracious gude Lord Ogilvy,' Sheriff-Principal of Angus; Sir James Scrymgeour of Dudhope, 'great constable of fair Dundee,' and good Sir Alexander Irvine, 'the much renounit Laird of Drum, nane in his days was better seen.'

Then there was Sir Robert Davidson, Provost of Aberdeen, who left his tavern in the Shiprow, gathered his burgesses around him, and set off to Harlaw to fight the cateran who were threatening his city. He died on the field of battle and his body was carried home by his comrades. The approach to the city of the cortege was described in a poem by Norval Clyne:

> 'Twas the same band, returning all,
> The living and the dead; for there
> The frequent corpses to the wall
> Their wounded comrades feebly bare;
> And there, unvisored, pale and dead,
> Stretched on his steed, where torches shed
>   A dim and fitful ray,
> The Provost came, and o'er him spread
> The town's broad banner lay.

When it was all over, they said 'ye'd scarce kent wha had wan.' I went away from the 'sair field' of Harlaw thinking of the last verse of the ballad:

> Gin ony body speer at you   *ask*
> For them ye took awa,
> Ye may tell their wives and bairnies
> They're sleepin at Harlaw.

13

CAMIESTON

The sound of battle drifts down the years from the Harlaw fields. An oddly-named stone sticks up from the ground as a reminder of another forgotten conflict . . . a signpost points the way to Clovenstone Farm (did the De'il's cloven hooves make their mark there?) . . . and the massive ruin of Hallforest Castle glowers out from another field. It seems to be all gloom and doom in the Garioch, and the only thing likely to put a smile on people's faces is – well – a goose!

I stood on the doorstep of a house near the Camieston farmhouse. The farmhouse and other buildings are now occupied by Thainston mart employees, and in front of me the mart fields stretched as far as the eye could see. Somewhere out there was a standing stone from which the farm had taken its name. It was like looking for a needle in a haystack, and I remembered the author Nigel Tranter saying 'it could not be discovered'.

Ian Reid, whose house overlooks this great sprawl of grassland, pointed it out to me. I could see why Tranter had missed it, and even when I made my way across the field it didn't seem much of a stone. It was upright, broad and sturdy, but just 5 feet high. About half a mile west of it was another flat stone, 4 feet square, lying on the ground. It was called Camie's Grave.

So who was Camie? William Alexander said in his *Place-Names of Aberdeenshire*, 'Tradition has little to say except that Camie fell here.' One theory is that his name was Camus or Cambus and that he was a Danish general. Alexander quoted as 'the ultimate authority' the historian Hector Boece, who apparently told of a Danish invader, Camus, who was defeated

The Camieston.

at Barry, Forfar. 'The place quhair he was slayn is callit Camistane.'

George Buchanan wrote about 'a great battle' that took place at Barry between Malcolm II and an invading force of Danes under a Viking called Camus, who was defeated and slain. It was said that a burn on the battlefield ran red for three days and the tumuli in the area are said to represent the large numbers buried from the battle.

Just to complicate things, there was another contender for the Camus crown, for on the Panmure estate in Monikie there is a Camus Stone, or Cross, which is alleged to mark the grave of the Danish viking killed in 1010. This stone, however, is said to be 'wholly Christian' and of a later date.

James Macdonald, in his *Place Names of West Aberdeenshire*, dismissed any theories about the Camiestone at Thainstone. He said there were several Camiestones in various parts of the country and a more likely derivation was the Scots word *camy* or *camie,* which means crooked or bent. 'It may be these stones were march stones, erected intentionally in a bent or sloping position,' he declared. The Thainstone Camiestone is neither bent nor sloping.

There are no such doubts about the Cloven Stone. This stone is a big split boulder near Clovenstone Farm, which serves as a march stone of the burgh lands of Kintore. This was where the court of the royal burgh of Kintore was held, and, while there were no cloven hooves clumping through the night, there was a whiff of Auld Nick there in 1596. That was when Isobel Cockie was condemned to be burned for witchcraft because, it was alleged, she had 'rossen [roasted] to death' a man who miraculously recovered by drinking from a holy well.

Less than a mile south of Camiestone as the crow flies is Hallforest Castle, a ruinous keep built by Robert the Bruce for Sir Robert Keith, Great Marischal of Scotland, as a reward for the part he played in the struggle for independence. Keith originally took the English side, but at Christmas 1308 he deserted Edward and joined forces with Bruce. His cavalry charge at Bannockburn in 1314 scattered the English archers and helped to bring victory to the Scots.

The historian W. Douglas Simpson, writing in 1923, said that castles of this period were very rare and the tower of Hallforest was 'an excellent example of the special type of military structure evolved during those grim and lean years of turmoil.' It replaced the stately piles of the vanished Golden Age, and in their place came 'simple, unadorned, grim, rectangular tower houses.'

The tower was four storeys high, with walls 7 feet thick. There was no drawbridge and instead of a stair there was a ladder, which the men used to enter the second storey, drawing the ladder up when they were inside. The castle was involved in the Covenanting troubles in 1639, when it was 'plundered by the royal forces under Lord Aboyne.' By all accounts the intruders showed considerable restraint:

> The soldiouris enteris, plunderis muskattis, guns, and other armes within the samen; brakis up the girnells to sustein thair army, yit wold not plunder nor tak any of the country peoples goodis and geir, which was put in this castell for preservation and keiping in thir troublesome tymes, bot ilk man cam and receavit bak his awin without harme or prejudice, quhilk wes noblie done.

In 1665 Hallforest was abandoned and fell into decay. 'The castle is now entirely neglected and in lamentable decay,' wrote W. Douglas Simpson.

'The wall-heads are in a bad state, large masses have fallen, and shrubs rooted in the upper portions will soon bring all to the ground.' That was eighty years ago and this architectural dinosaur still stands, defying time and the elements. It was built on low ground that would have been marshy and defensible. Now it is a field where hay is lined up along a dyke, heaped up for future use.

It is a formidable building, its masonry rough coursed rubble in local granite. If its ancient stones could speak it would no doubt have a tale to tell that would hold you to your seat. There is one intriguing story told about Hallforest long after King Robert had gone. It is said that during the reign of James II a traveller called at a house in Kintore and asked the occupant, a man called Thain, if he knew anything about the family at the castle. When Thain said, 'Yes,' he asked him if he would carry a message to Willie Keith.

'Willie Keith!' exclaimed Thain angrily. 'A better man than you would have called him Lord William Keith.'

Nevertheless, Thain delivered the 'message', which consisted of 'a knife and fork so constructed that the handles fitted into each other and appeared to be one, the blade and prongs being covered by a single scabbard.'

Lord Keith told Thain that the visitor was no less a person than the King. He was so staggered by the news he had to be accompanied home.

His wife, Margaret, suspected that the visitor was more than he seemed to be. While her husband was away she had a goose dressed for his supper and sat him down in the best chair. For this service, the king granted Thain a piece of ground designated in the title deeds as the Goose Croft.

Thain's house stood on or near the site of the local Post Office and the story was first told in 1843 by William Smith, the Kintore postmaster, who was related to the Thains. Today, Goose Croft still holds a place in the Ordnance Survey maps.

14

CAIRN OF THE PASS

The Carnavalage is not a name known to many people. Back in the seventeenth century, when Sir James Balfour of Denmylne decided to name 'the Chief Passages from the River Tay to the River Dee over the Mountains,' his list covered no fewer than eleven routes, including the Cairn-o-Mount, the routes from Glen Clova and Glen Esk to Glen Muick and Glen Tanar, and 'the Carnavalage from Glen Shee to Castle Town in the Brae of Mar.' Today, thousands of motorists driving over the pass know it as the Cairnwell.

The name is said to have come from a well, Tobar Chuirn, on the summit of the road, where Queen Victoria stopped to drink on her way to the Cairn an Tuirc plateau, but it was argued by some that the name had nothing to do with the well. Ironically, the well is now under the top car park on the Cairnwell Pass. The real name, apparently, should have been *Carn a' bhealaich*, 'the cairn of the pass'.

This ancient pass is the highest carriage road in Britain. How well used it was can be seen from the fact that there was a hospice there centuries ago. 'Ther was an Hospitall at Carnwall (called Shean Spittal, or Old Hospital), wher ther is a road over the Grampian Hills,' said the *View of the Diocese of Aberdeen* in 1732. ''Tiz said ther were several other such hospitals for poor travellers passing over Granzbin.'

After the Jacobite rebellions the road became a recognised route from Perth to Fort George and its importance grew when it became a military road. In 1864 the ten miles of road from Cairnwell to Braemar was reconstructed, with Prince Albert throwing in a contribution of £2,400.

The dark shadow of the cateran fell on the old pass in the sixteenth and early seventeenth century. 'Those wild scurrrilous people among quhom ther is bot small fear or knowledge of God,' Sir James Balfour called them. The cattle thieves came 'under cloud and silence of nycht'. Some raids were on a large scale. In 1602, men from Glen Garry raided the grazings in Glen Isla and Glen Shee and drove off 2,700 cattle. The men of both glens went in pursuit and overtook them in a place at the top of the Cairnwell known as the Caterans' Howe. There, the cateran fled, leaving their spoil behind them.

In a bid to bring a halt to cattle thieving, the authorities put small military detachments at various points from which the cateran made their incursions. Glen Feshie and Glen Clunie, Glen Muick and Glen Clova were key points. A Memorandum of 1747 detailed the routes by which stolen cattle were driven north by the raiders. They went through Glen Clova, Glen Callater and Glen Cluny to Deeside and up the south side of the Dee to the hills of Atholl, or they crossed the Dee below Invercauld and vanished into the passes of the Cairngorms

In 1689 there was a raid by 'a dozen wild Lochaber men'. They came down to the heart of Aberdeenshire – more than a hundred miles – and 'lifted' six score black cattle. They were pursued by fifty horsemen, each carrying bags of meal and other provisions, which they were to offer the raiders as ransom for the cattle.

The chase took them to Loch Ericht, into the heart of the raiders' own country, and at nightfall they were found encamped at Dalunchart. The offer of ransom – a bag of meal and a pair of shoes for each man – was rejected and the two sides fought it out. All the Lochaber men were shot down, killed or wounded, except three, who escaped unhurt. The cattle were recovered.

When the reiving days were over a different breed of men followed the old trails through the hills – drovers. In 1766, English cattle dealers started to come to markets in Scotland in search of beasts. There was a steady demand for Scottish cattle and the Scots themselves got into the game. The numbers of cattle brought to the trysts at Falkirk and Crieff increased steadily.

It was estimated by Sir John Sinclair, in the *Statistical Account of Scotland,* that about 100,000 head of cattle were sent to England yearly from Scotland towards the close of the eighteenth century. Some 3,000 were taken from northern districts to markets in the south, driven all the way by land from Caithness. About 8,000 to 9,000 were driven yearly from Aberdeenshire.

With the passing of the droving era, a splash of colour disappeared at the trysts. The scene at the Crieff tryst in 1723, described by a contemporary writer, showed drovers – 'mighty civil gentlemen' – dressed in slashed waistcoats, breeches, a plaid for a cloak and a blue bonnet. 'They have a poinard, knife and fork in one sheath hanging at one side of their belt, their pistol at the other and their snuff mull before with a great broadsword at their side.'

There are no blue bonnets and slashed waistcoats now on the Cairnwell, no cattle bellowing their way through over the pass; only coaches and skiers in woolly bonnets and cars crowding the car park where the Tobar Chuirn well is buried. Even Auld Nick has slipped into the mists. Whatever the name of the old pass, Carnavalay or Cairn of the Pass (the Hill of the Bags was also considered), it became almost irrelevant, for the only name of any importance to travellers was the Devil's Elbow.

The Devil has always reached out his horny hand to remote corners of Deeside. He left his mark on the Devil's Punchbowl on the Quoich, stirred his bubbling pot in the Devil's Kitchen in the cliffs above Loch Callater, and glowered down from the Devil's Point in the Lairig Ghru. It was said that the name Devil's Point actually came from *Bod an Deamhain,* 'the penis of the demon', but our stuffy Victorian ancestors kept that quiet.

But it was on the Cairnwell that the Devil did his worst, striking terror into the hearts of unsuspecting wayfarers. The Elbow was a one-in-five hairpin bend which motorists had to face when going over the Cairnwell and down to Braemar. Up on the Devil's Elbow car engines would groan and tyres would screech; nervous drivers wondered if they would slip downhill and end up where they started. Some cars went up the hill backwards, for the only way they could get over the Elbow was in reverse, which was the lowest gear.

Robert Anderson, editor of the *Aberdeen Evening Express*, wrote a book in 1911, *Deeside*, which described the Devil's Elbow in its heyday. The road, he said, was one of the most delightful coach drives in Scotland.

Eight or nine miles out of Braemar the road crosses a hill called the Cairnwell by a series of steep zig-zags with acute turns, one part, known as the Devil's Elbow, having a gradient of 1 in 9. Always hard upon horses, the Cairnwell road has been found in these later days no less trying for automobiles, and in consequence it has been occasionally selected for motor-car trials.

TAKING THE DEVIL'S ELBOW, GLENSHEE, THE HIGHEST PUBLIC ROAD
IN GREAT BRITAIN, ALTITUDE 2199 FT. ABOVE SEA LEVEL. A.8455.

Bus on Devil's Elbow.

With the development of motoring, the road has assumed a new importance, it being the only route from the south to Deeside; and it has recently been scheduled as a trunk road by the Imperial Road Board, who propose to make a large grant towards its widening and improvement, so as to fit it for the heavier traffic that now passes over it.

The Elbow has always been regarded as part of a road built by General Wade's successor, Major William Cauldfield, but in fact it came into being long after the military road builders had gone. Thomas Watson, hotel-keeper at the Spital of Glen Shee, and his sister, Mrs Clark of Invergelder, who took over the Invercauld Arms in Braemar in 1829, wanted to run a coach service from Perth to Braemar. The old military road was unsuitable for coaches, so they decided to improve the road at their own expense. So the Devil's Elbow was created and the coach service operated from 1829 to 1922.

Hamish Brown wrote in his book, *Hamish's Mountain Walk*, 'The famous Devil's Elbow is, alas, no more, being superseded by a foul steep brae which is much harder on cars.' Another writer, Ivor Brown, in *Summer in Scotland*, described the Cairnwell Pass as 'that absurdly courageous road that goes switch-backing up to the water-shed above Spital of Glen Shee and Dalmunzie House and then sweeps down beside the tumbling Clunie Water.'

The Cairnwell Pass had two hospices serving it, one at the Shean Spittal in Glen Clunie, the other at the Spital of Glen Shee. The last time I was there I was thinking of how it had been in the pass in the old days. In the first half of the eighteenth century it was little better than a cattle track and people went over it on horseback or on foot, but in the nineteenth century four-in-hand coaches were struggling up the hill. Now, cars and coaches go up and over bumper to bumper.

Back in the 1920s someone wrote a poem about the Auld Brig at Glen Shee and about the 'lumb'rin coach and creakin' wain' that crossed its 'humpit back.' Their days were numbered:

> Noo the cars an'charabancs
> Come birlin'up the road,
> And I'm growin' old and frail,
> An' canna thole their load.   *bear*

I have a feeling that the De'il is sitting up there on that 'humpit back' with a Satanic grin on his face, for people still talk about going over the Elbow – and the Devil's Elbow is still shown on Ordnance Survey maps. What it will be like in another century is anyone's guess, but I imagine that Auld Nick will be thinking of a way to torment the travellers of the future.

15

COMMANDER'S WARSHIPS

It was back in 1953 that Lieutenant-Commander Michael O.F. Forsyth-Grant retired from the Royal Navy. He never lost touch with the Senior Service. The names of famous battleships and destroyers were on his doorstep. He could walk on the Renown or the Revenge, and he could stand on Matchless and Musketeer and feel the sea breezes on his face.

He could do this because these were the names of fields on his estate at Ecclesgreig, St Cyrus. When he took over the estate, the old field names had been lost and he renamed them after ships in the flotillas in which he had served during the war.

Nowadays, fields are marked on maps simply by numbers, but this former naval officer regarded names as important. 'It is no good telling somebody to go and plough 0522483,' he told me. 'If you say Revenge or Resolution or Matchless they know what you are talking about.'

Ian Fraser, formerly head of the Scottish Place-Name Survey, once told me that farm field names were rapidly disappearing, partly because of farm technology and partly because the emphasis had switched to very large units. He was concerned that much of the field-name material in Scotland was in danger of being lost. Little had been done to gather field names in the North-east.

He echoed the point made by Lieut.-Commander Forsyth-Grant about farm workers being told to go to numbered fields instead of going to Gibby's Neuk or the Cocket Hat, Starvation, or Duncan's Park. These were real names, said Ian, culled from the thousands gathered by the

Place-Name Survey. They all meant something. The Cocket Hat was a triangular shaped field and Starvation a hard, unyielding feu, while Manitoba indicated that the field was flat. For North-east farmers there could be little doubt about the pungently-evocative Sharnyside, the name given to an old cow byre.

From field names the skilled researcher could find out about the vegetation and the wild life on a farm, what sort of livestock the farmer used and where he got his cattle from. Women were less good at the collecting game than men. The menfolk had walked the ground, worked sheep and cattle on it, and even poached over it. Yet it was women – members of the Scottish Women's Rural Institute – who gave the Place-Names Survey a boost by running a local history and place-names competition.

Ten years have passed since I first saw Ecclesgreig. Much has changed since then. In November 2000, the *Scotsman* reported that Ecclesgreig Castle was to be turned into a million-pound hotel and leisure development. Planning permission was granted but the plan was never implemented and in 1994 the application lapsed. Later, the estate and castle were taken over by Farquhar Estates, who planned a smaller but more realistic development. Their application was turned down.

When I went back to St Cyrus in 2003 I heard of the changes. I found Gavin Farquhar, head of Farquhar Estates, in his office in the castle, which hides away in a wooded hill overlooking the village, its shuttered windows and turrets hinting at its lost elegance. But one corner of the castle grounds held out hope for the future. Ten years earlier, the garden had been a jungle, wild and neglected, gloomily in tune with the sombre pile above it. It was a far cry from the splendid Italian Renaissance garden that had once been there.

Now, however, a new garden had arisen, laid out with professional skill. It was a joy to see. The art of topiary had sculpted bushes into shapes of unexpected beauty and statues had been brought over from Italy to lend style and dignity to the scene. In the middle of all this was a revolving summer house, which could be turned to face the sun, and on the edge of an adjoining wood was a gazebo, bought by Gavin for a song. Nearby, on a track coming out of the wood, were two pillars from a well-known hotel – a forerunner, perhaps, of Gavin's plan to recreate gate wells and posts at gate lodges planned for the estate.

These were innovations for the future, but what held my eye was something that seemed older than time itself. It stood near a short flight of

Gavin Farquhar in the grounds of Ecclesgreig Castle.

steps above the garden area, a Goliath of a tree, a cypress tree, with a monstrous trunk and great gnarled branches reaching out as if to warn you off, which, considering its age, would have been understandable. 'It's 900 years old,' said Gavin. Ecclesgreig Castle was built in 1844, but the lifespan of the castle seemed a mere flicker of an eyelid alongside the nine centuries that the cypress tree had survived. In a sense, it symbolised Gavin Farquhar's aim in life, which is to hold to the past and learn from it. That is what he does. He operates a historic buildings consultancy, working with bodies like the Scottish Civic Trust in what he calls 'architectural salvage.'

Ecclesgreig was an estate of some distinction. In 1821 it had a hundred servants and twenty gardeners – and a hundred dogs in the kennels. It is ironic that his efforts to 'salvage' his own castle have been frustrated by the grinding wheels of bureaucracy. He feels that action must be taken now to save what is still recoverable; income, he says, is needed for essential maintenance on the castle and on restoration of the grounds and policies to their former glory.

As we walked round the castle he pointed up to one of the towers. 'The Witch's Hat,' he said. In Michael Forsyth-Grant's time the tower was in a state of decay, but to restore it would have been an expensive business and the laird told the workmen what to do. The result was a new tower that looked exactly like a witch's hat. If there is a witch underneath it she may weave a spell that will take Ecclesgreig out of its troubles.

The old laird, however, is now well away from estate problems, for I learned when I went to Ecclesgreig that he had died since my last visit, which meant that the Renown and Revenge, the Matchless and Musketeer, had finally lowered their colours. Gavin Farquhar had known him well. They often came together in an evening to drink a dram and talk about the estate. It turned out that he was the author of three books, one on shooting.

The Commander was a keen shot. It was to Ecclesgreig Castle that the titled families of Angus and Kincardine gathered very year for the shooting season. He had odd ideas about field names and farm names and he changed the names of farms on his estate to the names of shooting estates he had shot over. For instance, Bowstripes estate became Invergarry,

Ecclesgreig Castle and its Witch's Hat

Gamekeeper's Cottage became Shieldaig and another farm ended up as Mount Pleasant.

This was a trait he must have inherited, for the name Ecclesgreig – the 'eccles' comes from the Gaelic *eaglais*, 'church' – was the result of name-swopping by his ancestors. It was originally known as the 'Lands of Mount Cyrus' and 'Lands of Criggie', but these names were changed to avoid confusion with the village of St Cyrus. An old map of 1774 shows the name of Criggie where Ecclesgreig now stands. The 'castle' replaced an old mansion house and was given the name Mount Cyrus – the Laird was William Forsyth-Grant of Mount Cyrus. A few years later it was changed again to Ecclesgreig. Oddly enough, Gavin knew nothing about the Commander's use of battleships' names as field names. He said that local folk still called them by the old names, for instance, Pleasant Field, Castle Field, Lang Field and so on, names taken from old title deeds and other documents.

Place-name addicts like myself often wander around old kirkyards studying the tombstones. They can yield some interesting names, and some puzzling ones, but there can be no more intriguing grave than the one I saw in the family burial ground of the Forsyth-Grants of Ecclesgreig. The grave was in memory of Osbert Clare Forsyth-Grant and the inscription on the stone read, 'Lost in the wreck of the *Seduisante* in Hudson Straits, 24th September, 1911.' No one looking at the grave would have known that it was empty.

Osbert was the son of Frederick Grant Forsyth-Grant, the Laird of Ecclesgreig. His uncle was Michael Forsyth-Grant. He had the sea in his blood like his uncle, but he had no thoughts of treading the decks of battleships. He had his eye on a different prey – whales. He had seen the whaleships sailing from nearby Montrose to the Arctic, or from Dundee, one of the great whaling ports in Britain. He had listened to the tales of old whalermen in Johnshaven and Gourdon.

In 1904, when he was twenty-four years old, he signed up for a voyage to Norway and Lapland and in 1905 his father gave him money to buy a ship with which he could join the Dundee whaling fleet. His whaler was a tiny ketch called the *Snowdrop*, the smallest vessel ever to sail with the Dundee fleet. His first catch was one black whale, two walrus and seventeen bears.

Four years later the *Snowdrop* went on its last voyage. It was battered unmercifully in a storm off Topjuack in Frobisher Bay and ended up a complete wreck. Osbert survived the storm and in 1911 bought a steam auxiliary, the *Seduisante*. It, too, was to have a tragic end. Nobody knows the full details of that last, ill-fated voyage, but it was thought that Forsyth-Grant was heading for Hudson Bay, where there were large numbers of walrus.

It emerged later that an Eskimo on the ship had sighted a herd of walrus and Forsyth-Grant had given pursuit, ignoring warnings from the Eskimos that they were in danger from rocks and shallow water. The result was that the *Seduisante* crashed into a hidden reef. The Eskimos were able to scramble ashore, but every member of the Scottish crew died. Only the bodies of the captain and the chief engineer were recovered.

For long after the sinking of the whaler there were stories of what happened on that fateful day. It was said that there had been mutiny on board the ship, that shots had been heard (there were shots, but they were signals asking for help), and that bullet-ridden bodies had been washed ashore. Whatever the truth, Osbert Clare became a legend in Eskimo land.

So the empty grave lies undisturbed, and life goes on in Ecclesgreig. There are names in this corner of the north-east that would delight the hearts of place-name collectors. Ecclesgreig was also the official name of the parish, but it was dropped in the 1790s and renamed St Cyrus. One of the houses in the village was called Genesis because Genesis was the first book in the Bible and this was the first house in Roadside, which, along with the hamlets of Kirktown and Burnside, were merged into one and called St Cyrus.

The Slunks is a ragged saltmarsh where the North Esk tumbles into the sea, and the Steeples is a semi-circle of basalt cliffs frowning down on the old kirkyard of Ecclesgreig, the 'church of the rock'. Go out and about and you will see the Smiddielands, or the Sillycots, and you will come upon Balwyllo, Glenskenno and the Land of Sands. The name that sticks in my mind is Mathers, for it was to a cottage at Milton of Mathers that I went with my family in those long-ago days when the sun always shone and I rattled about in an old Morris banger.

We often went down to the salmon bothy at Kirkside, where an old ice house was used by the salmon fishers. Salmon made St Cyrus what it is and it was salmon that gave it its name, for in the boom days of the salmon trade little Kirktown gobbled up Roadside and Burnside and produced St Cyrus. The red fish became a luxury trade through the foresight of George Dempster, the Laird of Dunnichen in Angus, who discovered a new way of sending his salmon to the London market.

In the winter, Dempster cut out blocks of ice from artificial ponds on his estate and stored them in ice houses through the summer. Then, instead of boiling or pickling his salmon he put them in wooden boxes with ice all round them for the journey to London. No one there had ever tasted fresh salmon from Scotland and the demand was enormous. St Cyrus was quick to copy Dempster's methods and three ice dams were built in the area, one of them an underground ice house built into the cliff.

The years slipped away when I went back to the Kirkside salmon station. The salmon bothy looked just as it had been a decade ago, but behind its white-washed walls changes had taken place. The Kirkside Bothy had become a guest house with six rooms, run by Ian Brake and his wife Mell, who previously had a similar bothy at Lunan Bay. There was also a café at one end of the complex, and above this was the Brake family's living accommodation.

But all that was to change. Not much more than a stone's throw from the bothy was the old ice house. Ian's plan was to restore the ice house and open a new restaurant in it, which would allow him to close down the bothy café and use the space there as extra accommodation for visitors. When I was there Ian and his son Clifford, who is nineteen, were working on the front of the ice house, where a conservatory was being added to the building to make a new entrance. Ian was previously project manager for a number of oil companies.

The land that goes with the Kirkside Bothy takes in the Nether Kirkyard. Here, the old Nether Kirk lies in a walled enclosure at the foot of

Ian Brake and his son Clifford at the Kirkside Bothy.

Ian Brake (right) working at the Ice House.

cliffs that provide an impressive background to one of the loveliest beaches in Britain. Time stands still here. Close to the ruins of the medieval church is the grave of a general who commanded the Dragoons at the Battle of Waterloo, while a table-stone tomb shows a gentleman and his lady pierced and united by Death's spear. It is not the sort of place you would wish to be on a dark night, particularly if a storm was blowing as it did when George Beattie walked to his doom in the Auld Kirkyard.

Beattie was a lawyer-poet, a wit, a practical joker (he once removed all the street lamps from their lamp posts during the night) and an impersonater. He made a name for himself with a poem 'John o' Arnha', all about a fearsome kelpie in the Pondage Pool and how John conquered it:

> Behind, a dragon's tail he wore,
> Twa bullocks' horns stack out before;
> His legs were horn wi' joints o' steel,
> His body like a crocodile.
> On smelling John he gie'd a scoil,   *squeal*
> Then plung'd and gard'd the water boil.

John o' Arnha was based on a town officer called John Finlay, who was a

The Nether Kirkyard, where George Beattie was buried.

familiar figure in Montrose with his red coat, knee breeches and broad-brimmed hat – and splay feet. Whatever his looks, he did well in the marriage market, for he was married five times. When he was asked which wife he liked best he replied that he 'aye liket the livin' ane.'

George Beattie wasn't so lucky. He 'liket' only one woman, the daughter of a local farmer. He had arranged to marry her, but her passion for the poet cooled when she inherited a large sum of money. She jilted him for a prosperous corn merchant. The discarded lover wrote a long poem, in which he told her she would soon be rid of him:

Farewell, maid, thy love has vanish'd
  Gone off like the morning dew.
Farewell, maid, my peace is banished,
  Adieu! a sad, a long adieu.

Weary world, I now must leave thee;
  Sun and moon, a long farewell;
Farewell, maid, no more I'll grieve thee,
  Soon you'll hear my funeral knell.

Beattie wrote to his lost love, hinting that suicide was in his mind, but she didn't believe him. He went to Aberdeen and bought a pistol. On the night of 29 September 1823 he spent some time in the inn at the Kirktown and then went down to the beach. It was a night for 'ghaists and spectres'. A storm broke over St Cyrus, the wind howling across the sand dunes and beating itself out against the cliffs. Beattie passed the salmon bothy and saw that there was no one in it, so he took out his pistol and fired a few shots at its door. He then walked along the foot of the cliffs to the old churchyard.

The kirkyard, crouching under the cliffs, is entered by an ancient stile with stone steps taking you over a rough wall. He sat down there, thinking, perhaps, of the final lines of his farewell poem:

> Gloomy grave, you'll soon receive me,
>   All my sorrows here shall close.

No one would have heard the shot in the storm that raged that night, but next morning a herd boy called Willie Balfour found him propped against the dyke close to the stile, with his hands on his chest, a pistol at his mouth, the thumb of his right hand on the trigger. He had blown his brains out.

His friends erected a granite monument over his grave a year later. It is near the spot where he died, enclosed with a stone wall and a heavy iron railing on top. The inscription on it reads:

To the Memory

of

GEORGE BEATTIE,

Writer in Montrose,

who died 29th September 1823,

in the 38th year of his age,

THIS MONUMENT WAS ERECTED

by the Friends who loved him in life

and lamented him in death.

For years after Beattie's death, people flocked to the Nether Kirkyard to see his grave. The Montrose author Duncan Fraser described it as a 'sentimental pilgrimage', which suggests that there was a good deal of sympathy for the rejected lover. Fraser said that Beattie had forgotten one inescapable fact – 'that the sons of humble crofters did not marry the wealthy daughters of country gentlemen.' No doubt many people were drawn to the kirkyard by a morbid interest, but now, nearly two centuries later, it has become a holiday attraction. There is a board in the graveyard telling you about it and about Beattie's suicide.

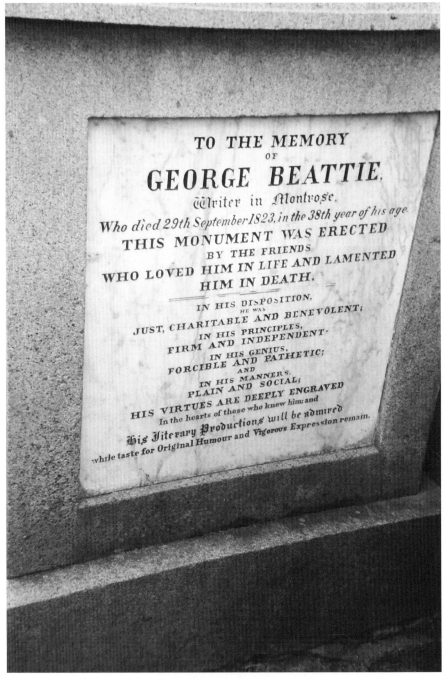

George Beattie's grave.

16

AN ESKIMO IGLOO

A wooden sign stands on the dyke of a farm road in the Deeside hamlet of Migvie. 'Coldhome,' it says. Beside it, as if to emphasise the message it carries, is a sketch of an Eskimo's igloo. Here, the air gets chillier as you climb up the track on Kirk Hill to reach the farm of Coldhome.

I stood gazing at the sign, wondering who had killed off a good north-east name that said far more than its successor. 'Cold' is bearable. 'Caul' is a raw, knife-like attack on your very bones. As the Buchan poet John C. Milne put it, 'bare an' an bleak an' cauld like the coast around ye.'

There are, however, precedents for Coldhome. James Macdonald, in his *Place Names of West Aberdeenshire*, went back to records of 1696 and found a Coldhaugh *and* a Coldholme. 'Coldhome generally means a house in an exposed situation,' he wrote. That is certainly true of Migvie's Coldhome, which sits on a lofty perch on Kirk Hill looking out over a breathtaking panorama of green field and hazy hills.

Nobody knows how Cauldhame became Coldhome, but it has been there for a long time. Bill Clark, a retired farmer, was in Migvie from 1929 to 1987 – farming at Coldhome. He started on the farm when he was seventeen years old. I tracked him down to Logie-Coldstone, where he has been living for the past fifteen years. Bill didn't know how the farm was given the name Coldhome, but, he said, 'We still ca'd it Caul'hame.' What made it so cold? 'It's on top o' a hill,' said Bill, with a shrug of his shoulders, but he didn't think it was *that* cold. 'There's another farm ca'ed

This signpost, with its igloo symbol,
can be seen in Migvie, pointing the
way to Coldhome Farm.

Bill Clark (left) and his neighbour Jimmy Birnie, who farmed at
Coldhome from 1929 to 1987.

Kirk Hill at the end o' the road that was far caul'er than it was at Coldhome.'

I had a sneaking suspicion that an earlier incomer from across the Border, faced with Cauldhame, had changed it, but when I went to Migvie and up the hill to Coldhome I found that an English woman was now living there. Michele Mort is from Cheshire and has been at Migvie for two years. She didn't agree with Bill Clark's view that Kirk Hill was colder. 'It can be freezing here,' she said, but admitted that the heating in the house wasn't as good as it could be.

Her partner, Lee Williams, is a gamekeeper on the Tillypronie estate. There was a stag's head, a twelve-pointer, resting against the wall outside the door. It was one of a twenty-strong herd of marauding stags that had been destroying crops. It was shot at the bottom of Morven and now its head was waiting to be cleaned and stuffed and hung in Michele's room. Michele loves this area. She has four youngsters, two boys and two girls. The oldest boy, who is eighteen, was with the army in Germany.

We stood looking across the great sprawl of countryside in front of us. Below, Migvie drowsed in an unaccustomed sun – Coldhome wasn't living up to its name. I could see where Migvie church, a plain, unpretentious building dating from 1777, snuggled up in a corner of the brae,

Michele Mort at Coldhome, with a panoramic view behind her.

overlooking a kirkyard full of old weather-worn tombstones. Left to drift into disrepair for many years, it was being renovated and painted, work that would turn it into a sanctuary.

Philip Astor of Tillypronie saw it as a place where people would find contemplation and spirituality. It was to be dedicated to his parents to celebrate their lives. Peter Goodfellow, whose Lost Gallery draws a steady stream of visitors to the wilds of Glen Nochty, was responsible for the panels that decorate the walls. They include one of Peter's paintings and panels carrying thought-provoking messages to people who visit the old kirk. I liked the one which read: 'The nature of God is a circle of which the centre is everywhere and the circumference is nowhere.' Peaceful little Migvie seemed the perfect setting for such a venture.

But I had other thoughts in my mind. I had gone to Logie-Coldstone in search of place names, or, more specifically, field names, and had found myself entangled in discussions about Cauldhames and Coldhomes. Now I had to put myself back on track by consulting Adam Watson and Betty Allan's classic book, *Place Names of Upper Deeside*, which gave a number of field names in Cromar. There were some interesting names among them. There was the Gallowhill Park at Auchnerran and the Tofts Park (a toft was a small patch of enclosed ground for rearing cabbages), and Ballabeg

Migvie Church

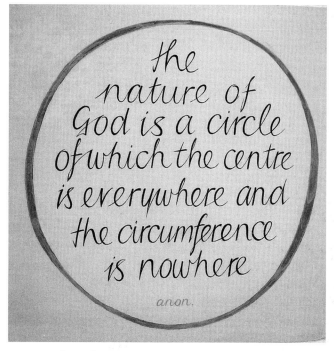

the
nature of
God is a circle
of which the centre
is everywhere and
the circumference
is nowhere

anon.

One of the panels in the Migvie sanctuary.

had the Front o the House Park and the Howmies. 'Howm', according to Chambers Scots Dictionary, is low-lying, level ground near a stream.

Twenty years have passed since the Watson-Allan book was published, and times have changed. On more than one occasion I found that an oil worker had taken over the farmhouse (and was away on the rigs) or that the house had been abandoned to the wind and the rain. Townhead was a ghost farmtoun, with no sign of life, the wind wheezing and groaning through desolate out-buildings and the farmhouse deserted. There were three field names for Townhead, two of them being the Gairden Park and the Wall Park, but there was no sign of a gairden or a well.

The third name was the Auld Wifie's Housie Park. It was a name that conjured up a picture of a little old lady sitting at the fireside, shawl around her shoulders, in a but-and-ben in the middle of a field. Who was she? Who looked after her? When was she there? I never found out, but when I drove away from Townhead I scanned all the fields in the hope of seeing the auld wifie's housie. There was nothing to see, not even a rickle of stones where it had been.

When I first saw Ian Fraser I discovered that not much had been done in the way of field name gathering in this North-east corner. I learned at Logie-Coldstone and Migvie that not many people knew any of the old names. Bill Clark and his neighbour, Jimmy Birnie, did their best, but with little success. Jimmy remembered the Hall Park, next to Newton Farm, which took its name from the nearby village hall. He worked at Newton Farm, he said, 'as a loon'. He was only fourteen then, now he is eighty-one.

The auld wifie in the housie made me think of the part women played in the place-name game. They sometimes found themselves in place-name rhymes. This one was from Corncairn, a district in Banffshire, not far from the Knock. It praised the thrift of its womenfolk:

A' the wives o' Corncairn

Drilling up their harn yarn,   *coarse cloth*

They hae corn, they hae kye,   *cattle*

They hae webs o' cloth forbye.   *besides*

Not all the rhymes were complimentary. In this one the Fochaber wives must have been tasting the hard stuff:

Aw sing a sang, aw ming a mang.

A cyarlin an a kid;   *old woman*

The drunken wives o' Fochabers

Is a' rinnin wid.   *mad*

Browsing through the place-name lists you will come upon ordinary women like Mrs Middleton and Mrs Shepherd. They appeared in *The Place Names of Upper Deeside*. The entries read 'Mrs Middleton's Puil' and what sounded like another auld wifie in a field – 'Mrs Shepherd's Park'. Mrs Middleton's pool was near the farm of Balintuim, south of Braemar, and Mrs Shepherd's park was 'a field east of Bridge of Gairn named after a former house on the site of the Craigendarroch.'

There were a few Megs and Marys in the Deeside list. Mary's Cottage was at Clachanturn, east of Crathie. Clachanturn once had a large and busy market, an inn, a smiddy and a ferry, and in about 1720 there was a school with eight pupils. West of Abergeldie there was a field called Mary's Cottage Park, not to mention Mary's Cottage Puil, which was also known as the Back o the House Puil.

Meg Wright's Hole was a boggy pool near Derry Lodge, where one of the servants fell in, and there was a Meggie McAndrew's Cairn near the Gairnshiel-Crathie road, which was erected after Meggie died in a snowstorm. A field at Inverey was called Jean Miller's Park and a field beside the former farm of Allt Mhor, north of the Pass of Ballater, was called Janet's Yard, after Janet Ritchie, the last person who lived there.

The Nells and Nellys held sway for a time. There was a Nell McIntosh's Cairn in Glen Lui, where a gale blew Nell off her bike about 1912 and at Aberdeen Haugh, south-west of the Inver, there was Nelly's Bothy. Nelly's Bush, a birch tree on the south bank of the Dee, had VIP status, for it was mentioned in Queen Victoria's diary. The queen had been out for a ride in her carriage with Albert. 'We got out at the river,' she wrote, 'and were going down to *Nelly's Bush* when a stag was heard roaring very near, so we had to stop.'

Not long ago I came across a field name that wasn't what it seemed – Isie's Croft. I discovered that there wasn't a croft, just a field. Isie was Isabella Duncan, who was born on a small farm called Candy Craig in Glentanar on 28 July 1883. That was the year that her father set out to reclaim uncultivated land on his holding. When he was trenching it he decided he would mark the birth of his daughter in a special way – by calling a field after her.

Little Isie Duncan grew up, married a Glentanar keeper called Willie Robertson, and become a grandmother. Her grandson, Bob Scace, who had emigrated to Canada, asked her to put down on paper her memories of her childhood at Candy Craig. The notes she wrote were put in a box containing letters and other correspondence sent to Bob by family and friends during his early years in Canada. The box was put in a cupboard and forgotten.

In February 2001, Bob opened the box when looking for letters written in the early 1960s. Inside the box was Grannie's manuscript. It was from this document, entitled 'Robertson Family History', that I learned about Isie's Croft. But that forgotten manuscript told me much more than the story of an unusual field name, for Isie had come into the world when a new laird was taking over the Glentanar estate – a wealthy Manchester banker and MP called Sir William Cunliffe Brooks.

'W.C.B.' was known for his eccentricity. He had his own ideas on what to do with names. He used his initials to put his name on one of the estate roads, Wilcebe Road – Will C.B. Road. Grannie Robertson's daughter, Mrs Betty Scace, who lives in Aberdeen, remembers her mother telling her how the laird played a magic trick on children, making them take pandrops out of his ear. He had other tricks up his sleeve. He put his initials on wells, seats, walls and stones all over the estate, along with cryptic homilies to passers-by. There were seven wells in Wilcebe Road, each inscribed with some message from Cunliffe Brooks. On one it read, 'Well to know when you are Well off.' Grannie wrote:

> I was born at the then small farm of Candy Craig on the 28 July 1883, The then proprietor was the Marquis of Huntly, Aboyne Castle. The marquis being a reckless spender of money, the estate came on the market for sale. It was bought by Sr William C. Brooks, a wealthy English banker, who set to work and remodelled the whole estate.
>
> He built new steadings and farm houses on all or nearly all of the farms. Ours was the first to be rebuilt. Our old farm house was built of stone walls and thatched roofs. No modern appliances of any kind in those days, yet when I look back I sometimes wonder if we weren't happier than the present generation with all the help they get.

When the house was built, Cunliffe Brooks asked the Robertsons to celebrate his birthday by sleeping in it. During the night, Grannie forgot she was sleeping in an open bed and not a box bed and when she turned over she found herself 'bang onto the floor'. Grannie was seven years old when the family moved to the new house. The old house stood in a clump of trees higher up the hills from the new Candy Craig, but all trace of it has gone.

A familiar name mentioned earlier in this chapter cropped up in Grannie Robertson's manuscript. This was a small field called Cauld Hame. 'The reason it was so named,' she wrote, 'was that there was a christening party passed that way going to get the baby baptized and on the way (they must have had a supply of strong drink with them) and feeling tired they sat down to rest and evidently took too much of the cratur (whisky). After they had got up and gone on their way for quite a distance they suddenly made the discovery they had left the child where they had been resting – hence the name Cauld Hame.'

This new version of an old tale may have been inspired by too much cratur. On the other hand, Isie's story came from a woman who had an iron will, who was very industrious and level-headed. It was more than likely that it was true.

Sometimes, however, place names can lead to confusion. The Place-Name Survey in Edinburgh once learned about a field at Dunbar in East Lothian called Jaws Field. It was thought at first that this was because the film 'Jaws' was showing at the local cinema. In fact, it went back to 1890, when a whale was washed up at Dunbar. Its jawbone was carried to a park and used as a gate. It eventually disintegrated, but the field continued to be called Jaws.

There are few new field names. 'There has to be some sort of trigger mechanism for the naming process,' Ian Fraser once told me. He named the naval line-up at Ecclesgreig as an example. So you have to draw back a curtain on the past, either through old farm plans, which many farms possess, or through old maps. I remember poring over a map at the Scottish Place-Name Survey's office in Edinburgh and reading, 'West side of Sandend Bay from a Plan of the Barony of Findlater 1761 by Peter May.' I knew Sandend well, for I have a friend who has a cottage there, but it was the name of a farm less than a mile from the village that caught my eye. It was called Brankanentham. James Macdonald thought it was 'pure Aberdeenshire Scotch', but what led him to this conclusion nobody knows. The word 'braankan' means gay or lively and Macdonald seemed to think that the name was an ironic comment on a bad farm.

The map showed fields with names like Brodie's Acre, Lady's Land, Meikle Tynnets and Duddie Buts. Duddie Buts suggests a field used for archery practice, but the old Scots word 'butts' also means a short piece of land. There was a watery butts near Turriff. There were also hills on Brankanentham, including William Wilkie's Chappell hill and George Ried's Chappell hill, and there was a field called the Swine's Snout. On the map it looked exactly like a pig's snout.

Across the disused railway that runs parallel to the road is the farm of Birkenbog. When I wrote about Brankanentham in a series of newspaper articles I received a letter from Mrs D. Clark, who lived at Birkenbog Cottage, Cullen. She told me that the Clark family had been in Birkenbog for more than 130 years. It was the home farm of the Birkenbog estate, which belonged to the Abercrombies of Forglen and Birkenbog.

Mrs Clark sent a list of the field names on the Birkenbog farm, giving the meaning of each name except two. One, the East Point, didn't require an explanation; the other was Rumbling Fall, which had a question mark after it. This was the list: the Deep (lowest field), the Stey Brae (steep hill), the Sheep Park (sheep preferred it up on a slope), the Rumbling Fall, the Jean Watt (an old lady had a little house there), the East Point, the Skates nose (shape), the Wall Park (a well or spring of water), the Oven Park (oblong shaped, with trees on three sides), the Garden Park (beside a walled garden), the Byre Park (behind the byre).

Mrs Clark was brought up on a farm on the same estate. Its name was Clashendamer and she wondered if I knew the meaning of it. The word 'clash' means a hollow or a ravine, and at a guess the second half of the word, 'damer,' probably had something to do with a dam, as in Clashencape, the hollow of the marsh.

I had a number of letters in response to the series, including one from James Duffus, who had just retired after thirty-two years working on the Fetternear estate at Kemnay. He set out a list of field names which had been in use since the 1930s. The estate originally belonged to the Leslies and one of the field names was 'Miss Leslies'. Most names were fairly straightforward – the Lang Dykes, the Barn Park, Little Drumfosk and Big Drumfosk, Broomhaugh, Barn Park, and so on.

17

THE LUMS O' GLASSLA

Cyaard, Cyaak and Cairnywhing,

An' scum the lums o' Glassla.   *scrape*

Ifirst heard that couplet from Roy Skinner, once the Grand Old Man of
the Buchan Heritage Society. A devotee of the poet J.C. Milne, he
travelled around Buchan lecturing to clubs and societies on Milne and his
poetry. It was when we were talking about old farm jingles that he said he
had heard the Glasslaw couplet as a boy in Boyndlie, where his father was
born and had a carpenter's shop.

J.C. Milne was Roy's hero. I used to send him a potted poem, written in
Milne mode, on his birthday. The last one was for his ninety-second
birthday. This is how it ended:

I telt the aul'man nae tae fash,   *trouble*

Yer the Skinner loon tae me,   *lad*

Ye'll plough a lang, lang furrow yet,

So gang on tae ninety-three.

The Skinner loon, as I called him, died in November 1995, less than a
month after reaching his ninety-third birthday.

Recently, I was reminded of those Glasslaw lums while reading a report
of a summer meeting of the Buchan Field Club in 1925. Some couthy
tales about the farmers at Glasslaw and Cairnywhing were told in a paper
by James Will, a past president. Oddly enough, one of the members

present at that meeting was R.T. Skinner, Edinburgh.

What particularly interested me was how the Glasslaw and Cairnywhing farmers were addressed, not by their names, but by their farms. William Duffus, the farmer at Netherton of Cairnywhing, was always called Netherton, or Ned.

'Did ye ever see the like o' aul' Ned the nicht?' said John Boyes, a New Pitsligo merchant, after some argument. 'He's terrible angry.' He reported a week or two later that it was all right. 'I hid aul Nedderton in the day afore yesterday for a lang crack an' a pinch o'snuff, jist the same's ever. . .'

The farmer at Nether Glasslaw was a Mr Pittendreigh, but he was best known as 'Glessla'. He liked to tell 'tall stories of the grossest kind.' Glessla's corn was so big you had to place a ladder against a thistle to see the field. Glessla's turnips were immense and his potatoes were 'marvellous'.

The practice of calling a farmer by the name of his farm was one of the topics dealt with in James Will's paper. It wasn't peculiar to Buchan, he said, but was common all over the country. Mains, Hillhead, Hilton, Milton, Nether, Midddle, East, West – these designations were easily dealt with, the occupants being styled Mains, Hillie, Middlie, Wastie, and so on.

'The names come glibly off the tongue,' wrote Will, 'but there are outlandish names of farms in the Buchan district . . . the spelling of which makes you pause and gasp.' He named some of them – 'Balquhindachy, Inverquhomery, Auchmunziel, Auquhorthie, Auquharney, Auquhath and Aucheoch.'

These are fascinating names to the place-name addict. Balquhindachy apparently had some connection with *coinneach,* moss, so it meant 'Foggietown' – in other words, we had another Foggieloan. Inverquhomery meant 'a junction of streams or roads'. Auchmunziel at New Deer was where the poet Flora Garry was born. From the Mains she looked across the landscape to Bennygoak, 'the Hill of the Cuckoo'. She said that the bird that gave the hill its name was 'yon bird ye niver see'.

Auquhorthie at Strichen was given a great skelp in William Alexander's book. The name appears as 'Aforthie' in Strichen kirkyard and Alexander said it was one of the most characteristic place names in North-east Scotland. There are, or were, at least half a dozen farms of this name and at most of them ancient standing stones could still be seen. Auquharney at Cruden came from *carnach,* 'the name of several places descriptive of rocky or stony situations.' Aucheoch at New Deer was from *ac fhiodhach,* 'bushy field'. Alexander mentioned a few places with bushy fields, including the Howe of the Auldyoch at Auchterless.

The use of farm names to identify farmers must have been embarrassing to some people. James Will wondered if there was any intentional humour in the mind of the person who first called the farmer of Balquhindochy Baldie. Other delicate contractions were Dumpie for Dumpston, Clubbie for Clubscross, Cockie for Cocklaw and Tummie for Auchenthumb. The most cringe-making name, in my view, lay on the shoulders of the farmer at Dumbmill at New Deer. He was called Dummie. Back in 1782 it was called Dummill, but it was changed for some reason or other to Dumbmill in 1795.

When I was checking these names in Alexander's *Place Names of East Aberdeenshire* I noticed a 'Dummies Howe' at King Edward beside Strocherie. The explanation given was far from satisfactory: 'It is said that at one time there were dummies living there.'

Will said that when names like Dumpie and Cockie were used they didn't suggest any underlying fun or absurdity, but this would happen if they were constantly repeated. A New Deer farmer, Andrew Clubb of Doghillock, used to tell of how he and a Mr Philip of Catcraig, Auchnagatt, were invited to tea in a Buchan farmhouse. The goodwife pressed them to eat and drink. 'Noo, Doggie, mak' yersel' at hame. Is yer tay sweet eneuch, Cattie?' On and on it went, until 'Doggie' had to put a stop to it.

In those days, the author of Pratt's *Buchan,* who was born at the Slacks of Cairnbanno, near New Deer, wasn't the only Pratt in the area. There was what became known as the Pratt colony – 'a group of highly respected farming families in the parish of Aberdour,' said Wills. Old John Pratt was the doyen of the group. There is a farm off the Tyrie road shown as Prattshaugh. It was also given as Prottshaugh, which was said to be a local form of Pratt.

Farmers had farm names, fishers had T-names. If farmers' names seemed odd, the fishers outdid them with names like Diddle, Dozie, Rounie and Pum. T-names were like jokes; you never knew who made them up or where they came from. Gladys Milne, in her book, *Bonnie Buchanhaven,* thought some people got them from their trade. 'Maist names,' she said, 'came fae gweed kens far' [God knows where].

The Banffshire Field Club, in its Transactions in 1916–17, carried an article on T-names which said that anything could give rise to a T-name. 'Many years ago a fisher lad was at the Neuk o' the Barns at Banff. "You're a gey birkie," said someone to him, and by Birkie he was known till the day of his death.' The word 'birkie' means a lively, smart youth.

The origin of the T-name goes back to the time when there was a proliferation of family names in north-east fishing communities, which meant a limit on the number of Christian names that could be used. For instance, take a look at the Banffshire roll of voters for the year 1914–15 and you will find that in the parish of Gardenstown there were sixty-eight Watts. Ten of them had Alexander as a Christian name. The T-names in the Watson clan ranged from Saunders' Son and Downie to Craik, Curly and Kitter.

Macduff had 17 McKays and 20 Wests and Cullen had 33 Gardiners and 55 Findlays. Portknockie had 20 Piries, 24 Slaters, 47 Woods, and 84 Mairs – in other words, 175 heads of families of four names. Findochty went one better. It had 182 householders with four names – Campbell 24, Sutherland 39, Flett 84 and Smith 35. 'The great tribe of Smith,' as it was called, certainly made their mark on this coast. No fewer than 26 of the heads of families in the little hamlet of Sandend belonged to the tribe. They must have been a clever lot in Sandend, for the T-name of three of the Smiths was Wisdom. The tribe was also prominent in Buckie, which had 116 Smiths.

'The great tribe of Smith' made their mark on the Banffshire coast in the old days. The Banffshire roll of voters for 1914–15 showed that 26 heads of families in the village of Sandend (above) were called Smith. Three of them had the T-name of Wisdom.

Today there is only a handful of Smiths in the village. I know Sandend well, for a friend of mine, Bob Bruce, has a cottage there. Bob was known as Katy's Teenie's Bobby. Katy was his grandmother and Teenie (Christina) was his mother. Sanyne, as it is known locally, has been swamped by incomers, mostly businessmen from the south buying up holiday homes.

Down the coast is Portsoy, which, as well as being the home of Portsoy marble, is noted for its pottery, porridge and potatoes. According to the roll of voters there was no great clan in Portsoy in 1914, for it could only boast 8 Mairs, 11 Piries and 14 Woods. But there are some interesting place names in the village, for instance, there are coastal rocks known as 'The Breeks,' where you can find the old vein of serpentine which produced Portsoy marble.

Cullen lies to the west, its two railway viaducts dominating the lower end of the town. The old voters' roll showed 33 Gardiners and 55 Findlays in the village, but there were some interesting T-names, such as Docker, Beamer and Hooker.

Bobbin was a popular name among the Mairs of Portknockie. Among them was a Bobbin Dandy and a Bobbin Shy, and among the 47 Woods of

The coastal rocks at Portsoy are known as 'The Breeks'. Here, you can find the old vein of serpentine which produced Portsoy marble. The old building with the red doors was a store overlooking the harbour.

Portknockie there were Wilken, Royal and King Cockie.

Two T-names caught my eye in that long list in the voters' roll – Budge and Smacker. Twelve years ago, when I was first researching T-names on the Banffshire coast, I came upon another, later Bodge and Smacker. The latter-day Bodge and Smacker were from the Murray clan, both with the Christian name of John, which showed why T-names were necessary.

Buckie is full of Cowies and Bodge and Smacker were discussing a George Cowie. The question was *which* George Cowie. The argument came down to whether it was George Codlin or George Pum. I don't think any agreement was reached on the matter.

I have often wondered what many of these T-names meant. Pum, for instance. Among the Jappys there was a Shake, a Prince Bodge and a Gyke. How did they come about? There were several with the T-name Latin and Portgordon produced a Gug and a Toddy. It is like a secret language. Wilma Aitken, who wrote a paper entitled 'Too Many Smiths in Portessie', said, 'A common feature of T-names is that it is seldom obvious how the name first arose.'

There is a story told about a stranger who went looking for an Alexander White – Sandy White – in one of the Buchan coastal villages. He knocked on one of the doors and a girl opened it.

'Could you tell me far Sanny Fite lives?' he asked.

'Fit Sanny Fite?'

'Muckle Sanny Fite?'

'Fit muckle Sanny Fite?'

Muckle lang gleyed Sanny Fite,' snapped the frustrated stranger.

'Oh! It's Goup-the-Lift ye're seekin', cried the girl, ''an fit wye did ye nae speer for the man by his richt name the first time?'

FOOTNOTE: There used to be a licensed house called the Sod Inn at the crossroads at Hillhead of Glasslaw. It was often simply called 'The Sod' and I wanted to find out why it got the name. There were a number of entries under 'Sod' in Jamieson's Scottish Dictionary. One gave its meaning as 'singular, odd, unaccountable, strange,' while another said it was a kind of bread, a roll made of coarse flour. Maybe they served up sod rowies with their beer.

Collins English Dictionary, on the other hand, said sod was a person considered to be obnoxious, or an exclamation of annoyance. It referred you to another entry, 'sod off', which meant 'to go away, depart'. I took the hint and headed for home.

18

ROWIN' IN A RIDDLE

I'd rather be on Loch Kinnord
Rowin' in a riddle,
Than here in Edinburgh town
Playin' on a fiddle.

There is a touch of Edward Lear about this Deeside place rhyme. Its principal character is a wizard. Like the Jumblies of Lear's nonsense poem, who went to sea in a sieve, he liked to sail about Loch Kinnord in a riddle.

Loch Kinnord, the popular nature reserve near Ballater, was once an eerie place, haunted by ghosts and peopled by witches and wizards. While the wizards sailed the loch in their corn-sieves, or riddles, the witches rode the air on their broomsticks.

But how did the wizard of the poem come to be playing a fiddle in Edinburgh? The story goes that he was Deeside's top magician, whose fame was known throughout the land.

When a great nobleman in Edinburgh heard about him he tried to secure his services, but the wizard refused. The only way of getting him to agree was to find an even greater magician who could cast a spell on him.

That was what happened. The Kinnord wizard was put into bondage and hired out to the nobleman in Edinburgh, where, as well as performing magic, he sang songs and played his fiddle at banquets held by his master.

The wizard was unhappy. He longed to be back on Deeside, but there is

Loch Kinnord, where a wizard went rowing on a riddle.

nothing to indicate that the story had a happy ending. Still, if you see a wizard sailing across Loch Kinnord in a riddle . . .

This story was told by the Rev. John G. Michie in his book *History of Loch Kinnord* 'as an example of the superstitious beliefs then entertained.' Michie said that the corn-sieves were divided into meshes by interlacing splits of wood.

The name Loch Kinnord has a confused origin. The correct name was said to be Kinner, or Kenner, and appeared in old writings as Keander and Canmore. Gordon's Map of 1654 showed it as Loch Keanders. William M. Alexander, in his *Place-Names of Aberdeenshire*, gave some old names around Loch Kinnord that were still known last century, although none can be found on today's maps. Flat land on the north side of the loch was known as Rinyac (horse pasture). West of there was a grassy flat called the Claggans, while the adjoining corner of the loch was Cra-Ellan. Others were Tambay (birch hillock), Kinnagarry (end of the dyke), a house called Carlochie, and a former croft called Presscow (hazel wood).

Gardiebane was given in Alexander's general list as a peninsula on the south side of the loch, separated from the land by an ancient rampant and ditch – 'a fortified site with its old name still attaching to it. On the other hand, *Jamieson's Scottish Dictionary* gives the word Gardy-Bane as 'the bone of the arm' and referred to lines from Skinner's *Monymusk Christmas Ba'ing:*

> He rumblet down a rammage glyde
> And peeled the gardy-bane
> O' him that day.

The poor chap who rumbled down the glide must have been badly hurt, for the word 'rammage' means rough-set, wild, violent.

19

THE PANDROP MINISTER

They called him the Pandrop Minister. His name was William King and he was minister of Glen Gairn Church for twenty-nine years, taking up his charge in October 1943. He would stand at the kirk door on a Sunday with a bowl of pandrops in his hand, offering them to his parishioners as they arrived for the service. The length of his sermon could be measured by how many pandrops you 'sooked'.

The folk who went to kirk at Glen Gairn would often jokingly ask the minister if it was a one pandrop service that day, or a two pandrop service. It was usually a one pandrop service. 'I've never had two pandrops,' said Dougie King, the minister's son, who went to his father's church as a boy. 'My Dad used to say it was never worth going on for more than twenty minutes.'

There is a book in the vestibule for visitors, full of praise for the church. One woman, who had come back to Glen Gairn after forty years, wrote, 'I came here as a child. It was lovely to be back in this beautiful place.' She added: 'And I still remember the pandrops!'

I had gone to Glen Gairn to see Dougie King's new house – the old schoolhouse. This retired teacher spent all his working life in Edinburgh but his thoughts often strayed to Gairnside and the old kirk, to the lofty hump-backed bridge and the gentle slopes of Mammie Hill. He took early retirement and in October 2002 he heard that the Schoolhouse was up for sale. He phoned Aberdeen to find out about it and discovered that the closing date was set for 4.30 p.m. next day. He immediately set off for the

Granite City – and put in his bid half an hour before closing time. He got the house.

The school itself had been converted into a home. Dougie learned that his neighbour was Hugh Inkster, a Deeside man who had been in the army for over forty years, returning to Deeside when he was back in 'civvy' street. His wife Helen, who is from the Ballater area, is a keen photographer. Dougie's wife Alison, better known as Ali, is a Londoner, a textile artist who does beautiful landscape tapestries as well as teaching in Edinburgh.

So life has livened up in quiet Gairnside, with new faces and new ideas, but I was looking for an old, familiar face when I was there. Rab Bain, who used to say 'I'm the last o' the Gairnsiders,' had told Dougie that he would come along to the schoolhouse at eleven o'clock that morning, but there was no sign of him. He would have some fine, unbelievable excuse, I thought. I went off with Dougie to see the ruins of an old corn mill on a little hill across the road from the church.

The mill, or what is left of it, stands above an area shown on maps as Kirkstyle. The mill dam is just above it. Dougie thought there had been a shop at Kirkstyle. The place-name expert William Alexander said that in Scotland the name Kirkstyle was frequently given to a place beside a

Dougie King at the ruined mill near Glen Gairn church.

church. Time and the elements have nibbled away at the old corn mill until only part of one gable-end is left, sticking up like some incongruous piece of sculpture.

A narrow path crosses the hill and drops down to the Shenval road. From the hill you can see three farms that Rab Bain leases for his sheep – Shenval (sometimes given as Shenbhal, from *sean-bhaile,* 'old burn') Richarkarie (*reidh,* 'field' or *ruigh,* 'shieling of Garchory) and Torran (little hillock). The Shenval farmhouse, for long a ruin, still clings to the edge of the moor. It is said that some woman bought it with the aim of moving it down the hill, but was refused permission. So *An Sean-bhaile,* 'the old farm town', rots away while cars and coaches grumble up the brae on their way to Corgarff and Tomintoul.

There is a curious flat-topped boulder on the hill, standing where Dougie and Ali often walk to in the evening to enjoy the view. There was also a mystery here. On the surface of the stone is a barely readable inscription – CML 1840. They say that the 'M' stands for Macgregor and that this was his grave. But the mystery deepened when we found another stone flat on the ground only a few feet away – and with the same inscription on it. It looked more like a gravestone, but why there were two stones and two inscriptions I never discovered.

When we were standing by the big stone a four-wheel drive vehicle came down the Shenval road, swung round below us, and stopped. The driver was Rab Bain, who had seen us on the hill. We shouted and waved and out he came.

'What happened to you?' asked Dougie.

'Ach!' came the reply, 'I jist forgot a' aboot it.'

He was the same old Rab, unshaven, dressed in a tartan shirt (with galluses) and a woollen 'tammie' on his head.

'How are you keeping?' I asked, as he came up the hill.

'Hingin' on by a thread,' he replied, and added, 'An afa thin thread!'

He has had his share of ill health and hospitals, having a quadruple bypass a few years ago. The first time he was in Foresterhill with a suspected stroke the consultant told him that he had given his brain an examination and there was nothing there. 'Good God!' said Rab. 'There must be something there. I've hid it for mair than sixty years!'

When he was a patient on another occasion he got fed up with his confinement and walked out. 'He just got up and pushed his way out,' said Dougie. But he picked the wrong door – and set off all the alarms in the hospital. Rab's explanation was short and to the point: 'There wis ower mony doors'.

Rab Bain with the author at the mystery stone.

He had his dog, Nap, with him on the hill and I reminded him of the time when he had Brush, 'a topper o' a dog', he said, who died of cancer when only eight years old. He used to say with a toothless grin, 'I've got twa teeth an' my dog has ae e'e.' I told him that a friend of mine had read that in one of my books and couldn't make head nor tail of it. She finally came to me and asked, 'What on earth does "ae e'e" mean?' She was English.

I watched him as he made his way down the hill, pipe in his hand, Nap at his heels. There are few like him nowadays. He still lives in his eyrie, a farm at the top of Queen Victoria's Roadie, high above Crathie and Balmoral. It was built for Victoria so that she could go up the hill in her gig. He still tends a flock of some 500 sheep, shearing them himself with some help from local lads. I was glad I had seen him again.

That day in Glen Gairn we roasted in a heat wave that lasted through the summer. There were other visitors when we were there. We sat round a circular table outside the schoolhouse, talking and eating a picnic lunch. In Dougie's sitting room I had seen a flaughter spade, a spade for cutting peats, and he told us that the minister was allowed to cut peat once a year. 'What a mess we made of it!' he said.

The minister was also allowed to fish in the minister's pool and in Pool

Mary and the Cock Pool, two in the Gairn and one in the Dee. 'We were shambolic,' said Dougie. 'Dad used to go out visiting people where he knew there were old rods.'

We talked about the minister's lot, which sometimes had its problems. Dougie recalled the time when his father was commiserating with a parishioner whose wife had died. He was in full flow when the man held up his hand and said, 'No, Minister, stop there. I never really liked the woman.'

Then there was what Dougie called 'a wee story about him loving the whisky.' This was when the trains were running. 'It was said that because he was a minister he didn't like getting his whisky from Collie's in Ballater, so he got it from Collie's in Aberdeen and had it sent out in the train. There was one time when the stationmaster rang up and said to Dad, 'Minister, your books have arrived – and one of them is leaking.'

The truth was that the Kings had no drink in the house. 'I almost never saw Dad drink,' said Dougie. 'He'd have a wee sherry now and again.'

Dougie and Ali were good hosts, but the day wound on and it was time to go. I left the glen reluctantly. Driving over the old hump-backed brig and down the Gairnshiel road I was thinking of some of the ministers who had been there before William King. There was, for instance, James Anderson Lowe, whose daughter Amy Stewart Fraser wrote about Glen Gairn in *The Hills of Home*.

More than a century had passed since James Lowe and his bride, Agnes Smart, drove up the Culreoch Brae in a hired waggonette on their way to their new home. Beyond Torbeg, they crossed the Gairn by a stone bridge that was later swept away in a storm of wind and rain. There were plans to have another cart-bridge built, but the money subscribed was sufficient only for a footbridge – the Black Bridge. Carts had to ford the river, as tractors do nowadays.

On their way to the manse, James Lowe named all the farms and cottages that they passed. Before long, he was to know virtually every ferm-toun and cottar house that lay in the shadow of Morven. He had a large parish, extending well beyond Glen Gairn. It took him to Micras, which was then a clachan, and down to the Braes o'Cromar. He had scarcely settled down in his manse – it was only his first week – when he tramped over Morven to Cromar. The following day he travelled six miles to baptize a shepherd's children and the day after that he was at a funeral in Crathie, which took two hours of hill-climbing each way. He wrapped up his week by going ten miles to baptize a baby at Morven.

His congregation must have thought they had a minister in a million, but Amy Stewart Fraser said her father was young and strong and thought nothing about it. 'For the next seven years,' she wrote, 'he footed it blithely till in 1898 both he and my mother were able to buy bicycles.' His trips through the hills to visit his parishioners were all entered in his log-books. I would liked to have seen them, for when I was researching old settlements on Morven I was conscious that I was walking in James Lowe's footsteps.

In Mr Lowe's time a shepherd called George Coutts lived at Bothanyettie with his wife and family. It was a lonely, isolated corner of the glen and he paid regular visits to the Coutts family. To get there he had to cross the Glenfenzie Burn at Mullach, a farm high on a hill above the burn, and make his way over the Hill of Lary to Bothanyettie.

The name Bothanyettie was said to mean 'the bothy of the juniper'. There were a number of *larachs* near the croft, many of them buried in the heather under a shroud of juniper bushes, hiding what had been a prosperous community. They had names like Loinn Mhor and Loinn Bheag, Bogmuick, and Glachantoul, the hollow of the barn. There were seventeen houses in Wester Morven in 1850, but nineteen years later, in 1869, the Ordnance Survey map showed only four of them, three in ruins. The others had vanished.

So how many habitations were there in Glen Gairn when the population was at its peak? Some light was shed on the matter in Adam Watson and Elizabeth Allan's *Place Names of Upper Deeside*. This indefatigable pair included in their work an appendix with lists of former habitations, leaving out names on current OS maps, electoral registers and valuation rolls, house names in villages and hamlets and shielings and shooting lodges.

They came up with some surprising figures. Up the glen to Gairnshiel there were forty-one habitations, while above Gairnshiel, an area virtually bereft of life, with the ruins of a few abandoned farms crumbling away on the hillside, there were twenty-seven. The lists showed places I had written about, among them Glen Bardy, the 'glen of the little enclosed meadow', where you can look back and see a stunning view of Lochnagar. Daldownie, Sleach and Corndavon were other names.

There were also curious names unknown to me: Half Bad Charn, a farm that later became part of Tullochmacarrick; Ruuigh Baile o' Chlaiginn, a former shiel west of Corndavon Lodge; Cossack, from Cosag, '*a little crevice*', and Croit Caluim, 'Malcolm's croft'.

The Hill of Morven lords it over all the little hills, but the more modest heights have always had a special appeal to me. The communities that were once scattered along Glen Gairn were cushioned by the wee hills, among them the Brown Cow Hill, which locals call the Broon Coo. Seton Gordon said there was often a large drift beside it, which lingered on until midsummer and was known as the Broon Coo's White Calf.

There was Torbeg, the little hillock, the Camock, 'hill of the crook', and the Ca', where an old trail went over the hills to Cock Bridge. Then there was Mammie, 'the rounded hill', which looks down on the crofts and touns between the Gairnshiel Brig and Lary. Lying in its lap are the ruins of another Ardoch, which was called the 'Metropoleon o' the Waterside'. Even in its hey-day it was said to be 'a nasty, guttery (muddy) place.'

Above Ardoch was Clachnaschoul (Clach nan Sealladh), the stone of the views, where a Roman Catholic priest, the Rev. Thomas Meany, often sat with his parishioners and listened to their tales. That was more than a century ago. 'It was a hairty ples!' said one old woman. It is a sad sight now. I remember sitting there, looking across Ardoch to where the Gairn swept imperiously down to the Dee, and trying to imagine how it had been in the good years when it was 'thickly populated,' bubbling with life.

'They were hardy, friendly, contented in the remote beautiful glen, where few influences from the outside world came to disturb the even tenor of their days. They were industrious, thrifty, contented, and kindly, and their lives were often brightened by flashes of real rural wit.' That was written by a daughter of the manse, not Amy Stewart Fraser, but Catharine Neil, whose father, the Rev. Robert Neil, came to Glen Gairn with his bride more than forty years before the Rev. James Lowe came to the glen with *his* bride.

Catharine recalled those far-off days in a booklet, 'Glengairn Calling', written in 1943 when the world was still at war. Amy Stewart Fraser's book, published in 1973 and running to 235 pages, became a best-seller, bringing the magic of the glen to thousands of people. Catharine Neil's booklet, with only twenty pages, had a limited readership, yet it gives a fascinating glimpse of the glen in an earlier era.

Robert Neil's first manse was a two-storey building at Tullochmacarrick, across the Gairn from the hamlet of Loinahaun. He was later given another house at Dalfad, three miles down the glen. It was from Dalfad that twenty-five Macgregors set out for Culloden in 1746. Many did not return, so that a little chapel being built in the wood nearby was never completed. There is an old burial ground there.

Catharine Neil crowded a surprising amount of information into twenty short pages. She told of the old men, still there in her time, who had brewed the barley bree, and who could tell of their adventures when, evading the exciseman, they slipped up the hills by Glen Doll with their little ponies laden with kegs of whisky. They knew well where to dispose of these.

A laird on the Forfarshire side tried to close the old drove road, but the Scottish Rights of Way Society took up the case and won it. Two witnesses from Glen Gairn were called to give evidence in support of the Rights of Way Society and one of them was asked if he went that way with sheep or cattle. He replied, to the amusement of the court, 'I was drivin' smuggled whisky, sir.'

She told, too, of the busy lives led by the farmers' wives. 'Their work was never done. From morning to night they toiled on milking cows, feeding calves, pigs and poultry, then making breakfast, baking, washing, cleaning, and cooking the simple meals, and many other items of household work. Then every house had a wheel, and they spun the wool from their own sheep for all the household clothing, and yarn to make wincey and serge. Then dyeing the wool was an art in which they were all proficient.'

She wrote about a weaver at Loinahaun who was always in demand for funerals. There was rarely a hearse. The coffin was carried on the shoulders of four men and the weaver walked in front giving orders when the tired bearers had to be replaced. He did it by calling 'Ither fower!' New bearers then stepped forward to take their places.

The school, which at one time was attended by as many as sixty pupils, was at Dalphuil, near the church. When it ceased to be a school it was known as the Auld Schoolhouse or the Teapot Cottage. It was bought by the royal family and became a playground for Princess Elizabeth and Princess Margaret. When the Education Act was passed in 1872 a new school and schoolhouse were built.

20

DULSE OF DUNNIMAEL

The dulse of Dunnimael
Maks sick fowk hale

Dunnimael is a rock just south of Stonehaven, where the sea comes churning on to the shore near Dunnottar Castle. There are three 'duns' or forts on this stretch of coast, the best known being Dunnottar itself. Dunnacaer, the 'little hill fort', which is on the southern tip of Strathlethan Bay, is where fragments of incised Pictish stones were found in the middle of the nineteenth century.

Curiously, a number of years later, they were thrown into the sea by the three youths who found them. One of the youths went back to search for the stones and discovered them completely covered with seaweed.

On the other hand, Dunnimael, the 'fort of the whirlpool', is known, not for its stones, but for its seaweed – the dulse that, according to an old couplet, 'maks sick fowk hale'. The gathering of seaweed was a popular activity along the north-east coast. The Bay of Nigg was a rich source for Aberdeen dulse hunters, as an old jingle testifies:

We're a'awa' tae Torry rocks,
Tae Torry rocks, tae Torry rocks,
We're a' awa' tae Torry rocks
Tae gather dulse and tangles.

The famous 'tangle o' the Isles' was noted for its health-giving properties.

On Stronsay, 'sick fowk' drank from the healing well of Kildinguie, and besides drinking the water also ate some of the dulse from the shore.

In modern times, dulse became a cure for economic as well as human ills. Seaweed factories in the Isles dried dulse, milled it to a fine grain, and sent it to the mainland for processing.

The chemical that is produced is used in the making of textiles, paper and ceramics, as well as foodstuffs such as puddings and jellies. It is also popping up as pills sold in health shops, where, like the dulse of Dunnimael, it continues to 'mak sick fowk hale'.

21

LIZZIE MURDOCH'S BIBLE

The Bible was small, only four inches long and two inches wide. 'New Testament' was printed in faded gilt across the front cover. For a long time it lay unopened and unheeded on a bookshelf in my room, but one day it was accidentally dislodged. It tumbled down on to my desk. When I picked it up I saw a faint, barely-readable inscription on one of the pages: 'Lizzie Murdoch, Aberdour House'.

Lizzie Murdoch was my mother. Although I had kept the Bible for many years, I had never noticed that faint signature – or the name of Aberdour House. I knew she had been 'in service' at one time, in Buchan and in Aberdeen, but I never knew that she had worked for the landed gentry in 'a substantial old-Scots house of great charm.'

I sat looking at that worn, faded Bible, wondering at this message that had dropped out of the past, thinking how little I knew about my mother's early life. She was one of sixteen sons and daughters, which was notable even in an age when big families were commonplace. I had forty-nine cousins on my mother's side. She sometimes spoke about her sisters and brothers, but never about her own childhood – and I never asked about it.

Now, I decided, I would go in search of those lost years. It would take me to Logie-Buchan and the Ythan, to farms and villages where my relatives had worked on the land or mended tackity boots in souters' shops, to the farm where she was born, to the old abandoned kirk where she had been baptised, and to Aberdour.

Her birth certificate was the starting point. It told me that Elizabeth

Lizzie Murdoch's Bible

Hutcheon Murdoch was born at 3.10 p.m. on 12 May, 1891 and that her parents were John Murdoch, a farm servant, and Agnes Murdoch, whose maiden name was Munro. They were married at Alvah, a small hamlet scattered across a hill in Banffshire, on June 7, 1878. Twenty-nine years later, my grandmother died at a farm at Tarty in Buchan. She was only forty-four.

When I was writing *Buchan, Land of Plenty* I went to Tarty, chasing ghosts, I suppose, but there was little there that connected me to my roots, although my grandfather had been grieve at Tarty farm and my mother a domestic servant. The name is said to have its origins in the Gaelic adjective *tabhartach,* meaning generous, but the relevance of that escaped me.

Tarty has always seemed to me to be a kind of Buchan Siberia. The very names make you shy away from it; the Sleeks of Tarty, for instance, a stretch of oozy mudflats which carts once crossed before a bridge was built; and the Snub (pronounced 'Snob'), a spit of land that is a haunt of wildfowl, and Inch Geck, an island which was said to be good for fattening cattle ('Geck' is the Scots word for fool).

I remember meeting a young Australian, Dave Skidmore, and his wife Tina, at the Howe of Tarty. In their first winter there they faced blizzard conditions, with frost and snow throwing an icy coat over the Ythan estuary. Their water pipes froze and broke up and had to be replaced, but they loved its isolation and its sense of tranquility. I could understand that.

The tinkers came through Tarty when, like the migrant geese, they were off to their summer quarters on a hill at Tyrie, their 'cairts' rattling down the road to the Ythan. They never lingered long in Logie-Buchan. Flora Garry wrote about it in one of her poems:

So they'll no deval by Tarty's waal,	*stop*
Nor daachle lang at Udny,	*dawdle*
The hedder hulls afore them lie,	*heather hills*
Their summer home Turlundie.	

I wondered what young Lizzie Murdoch had thought of Tarty and the Sleeks and the changing world around her. Life must have been hard for her, working as a 'kitchy deem' as her mother's life slipped away. She was left to bring up some of the younger members of the family.

My journey into the past began, not at Tarty, but at another farm a long way away. Its name was Raecloch, between Aberchirder and Turriff. It was there that my mother was born. They said that the farmer at Raecloch was always called 'Clochie,' so I went in search of him.

The farm is situated in woodland just off the B9024, about three miles from Turriff, not far from where the Deveron does a dizzy U-turn on its way to Marnoch. When I turned down the track to Raecloch I came upon a scene that stopped me in my tracks. I could barely see the farmhouse. 'Clochie's' had been swallowed up by a wilderness, and what I could see of it spelt ruin and desolation. The woodland had closed in on the farm, trees and bushes forming an impenetrable barrier between the track and the house. It looked as if a wooden porch, perched uneasily at the front of the house, was being supported by the trees. There was no path to the door; it had disappeared in the undergrowth.

Wildflowers and weeds were keeping the world at bay . . . stickie willies, dandelions and daisies, nettles that threatened your legs and briar roses that tore at your hands. I never saw 'Clochie's' place from the inside, nor did I go through the door of the house where I imagined my mother had been born. As far as I could see, this was the only other building on the farm. It was only a stone's throw from the farmhouse, near a beautifully-made slate dyke. Beyond the dyke was a steading, its roof gone, but there were two shattered gables – and there was life in one of them.

One of my companions on that outing was waving his arms to attract

The farm of Raecloch, strangled by trees and bushes.

my attention. He put a finger to his lips, warning me to be quiet, and beckoned me over. He pointed up to the shattered roof of the steading. Sitting in the corner was a barn owl, watching us with unblinking eyes. I always thought that owls appeared at night, and slept in the daytime, but it was a wide-awake owl that was looking down on me. It would have known all about 'Clochies.' It might even have heard stories about my grandfather, old Jock Murdoch, who had been a farm servant at Raecloch, and my mother, Lizzie Murdoch, who was born there and baptised at Marnoch. It was a pity that wise old owl couldn't speak.

I wanted to get closer to it, to have a look at it, so I pushed my way carefully through a barrier of nettles. There was a great flutter of wings and Mr Owl shot into the air and disappeared over my head. I left the farm and walked down the track to a field that ran uphill between the Bogs of Laithers and Ardmiddle Mains. Looking back, hoping for a last glimpse of the farm, I saw only the wood that had hidden it. I had seen the last of 'Clochie's'.

From Raecloch I went west, chasing the Deveron as it wriggled through some of the loveliest country in the north-east, speckled with mighty castles and impressive mansion houses. I was heading for two places that were closely linked, Aberchirder and Marnoch. Marnoch was where my mother was baptised and Aberchirder was where Foggieloan was born. Foggieloan was the original name of Aberchirder, and not, as is generally believed, its nickname. The name came from a croft on the site of the Fife Arms Hotel, where the village had its birth pangs. The parish was then known as Aberchirder, but in time its usage was confined to the burgh, while the parish became Marnoch, the church being dedicated to St Marnoch.

The modern burgh of Aberchirder was officially founded in 1764 when Alexander Gordon of Auchintoul announced in an advertisement that he intended to feu out part of his estate to form a village near the House of Auchintoul on the high road from Banff to Huntly. 'The place will be plentifully supplied with water,' it said, 'and the feuars can be accommodated with firing from the moss of Auchintoul.' Tradesmen, manufacturers and others were invited to apply to the laird.

Before that, the centre of parish activities was at the Kirk of Marnoch, a couple of miles from the site of the future village. The parish school was a short distance away. In 1790 the Statistical Account of Marnoch reported: 'The church is very old and in a ruinous condition. A new and much larger church is to be built.' The church was built on the Cairnhill in 1792. This was the site of a Stone Circle and one of its mighty pillars, dating back to about 1500 BC, still holds its place there.

The Marnoch Church stone.

But this corner of Marnoch, whose 'new' parish church was to have a turbulent history, gave way to the growth of Foggie. It is no longer the hub of activity on Deveronside. The church on the hill, which came to be known as Old Marnoch Church, closed its doors a few years ago, as did the school. Mabel Mutch, who was born in Aberlour and moved to Marnoch when she was five years old, lived in the one and only street in the area – Muriel House Terrace. She was there for fifteen years, and now lives in Glasgow. She was one of a family of seventeen, who made up the total Sunday School roll.

Old Marnoch Church stands on an idyllic spot, looking out over Deveronside. It is hard to believe that this peaceful scene was the setting for a titanic struggle that split the congregation and brought about a breakaway that ended in the building of a new church in Aberchirder. It all began with the appointment of a new minister. When the Rev. William Stronach died in 1837 the patrons, the trustees of the Earl of Fife, wanted a schoolmaster, the Rev. John Edwards, to take his place, while the congregation thought that the post should be filled by the Rev. David Henry, who had been assistant to Mr Stronach in his last years. The result was a bitter dispute that lasted for six years and led to the setting up of New Marnoch Church in Aberchirder.

Old Marnoch Church.

New Marnoch Church at Aberchirder.

On a wintry day in January 1841 some 2,000 people gathered at the church for a meeting that lasted all day, packing the kirk like sardines or standing outside in the snow. Edward's supporters, the so-called Intrusionists, were pelted with snowballs, pieces of bread, and copper coins and the day ended with the Marnoch parishioners walking out of the church for the last time. 'Old men with heads as white as the snow that lay deep on their native hills, the middle-aged and the young, joined together in this solemn protest,' said one report. They went down to the foot of the hill, where roads went off to Aberchirder, Ardmellie and the Manse, and in a little hollow there they held their first meeting after their virtual expulsion from the church.

They set up a new church – New Marnoch Church – in Aberchirder in less than a year and the Rev. David Hendry, the minister of the parishioners choice, was inducted. The congregation of New Marnoch called it a non-intrusion Church of Scotland and joined with the United Free and later with the Free Church of Scotland.

More than a century after the great walk-out, Old Marnoch and New Marnoch became a joint charge. Today, the doors of Old Marnoch Church have been closed for good. Unlike churches that have ended up as workshops or nightclubs, it has retained its dignity. I was given a key to get into it. I half-expected to find its empty pews a depressing sight, but it looked as it had always been, a place of worship with a quiet beauty about it. There was no sign of neglect; everything inside the old kirk was spick and span, almost as it had been made ready for the next Sunday service.

Upstairs in the gallery, I looked down on the seats where the parishioners had taken their places on that fateful day in 1841. The gallery had been reserved for visitors, but during the meeting one of the beams supporting the gallery began to give way and there was a panic-stricken rush to get out of it. But now, more than a century later, the church on the hill was showing its best face to the world. The empty pews below stretched away to a pulpit that no longer held a preacher; the silent organ stood near it, and in one corner I could see a baptismal font.

It was a reminder of why I had gone there, a link with another baptism that had taken place in Old Marnoch Church long years ago, for I was looking down on the spot where my mother was 'christened' in the dying years of the nineteenth century. In a corner of her faded birth certificate, registering her birth at Raecloch, the local minister had written in tiny sloping letters: 'Baptized the 6th Dec 1891 Geo. Johnston minister Marnoch.'

The parish of Marnoch is about eight miles in length and its greatest breadth is about five miles. The Deveron traces the southern and south-eastern boundary for about six miles, measured in a straight line, but it twists and turns so much that the distance along its bed would be at least twice that. There are some interesting place names in it. I saw one coming in from the west, Wettyfoot, and wondered if that held a weather warning. The ubiquitous Reekitlane was there and there were curious names like Loothcerbrae, Knobbygates and Knauchland. But the most puzzling name of all was waiting for me down in the old Marnoch kirkyard.

The Marnoch cemetery seems immense for this little community, but it is, in fact, the parish cemetery. Down in the low ground near the Deveron the original parish church, empty and deserted, still stands on the edge of the kirkyard. Row upon row of tombstones stretch away from it, over 700 of them. The names on the gravestones form a long roll call of families who have lived out their lives in the lands of Foggieloan – farmers, merchants, gardeners, blacksmiths, crofters, quarrymasters, tinsmiths, innkeepers, shoemakers, an endless list of occupations. Many were from Aberchirder. There were ministers there, too, among them the Rev. David

Henry, who, as the inscription says, died in 1870, 'after 30 years of faithful & devoted labours as first minister of Free Church in Marnoch'.

Windyedge, Deafhill, Brokenfolds, Quarryhill, Battlefield, Lythebrae, Damfolds, Skeibhill, Shargerwells . . . behind the names were countless untold tales, but one particular name stopped me in my tracks – Fill the Cap. The name on the gravestone was William McBain, but the lettering on the stone was obscured by lichen. Later, I found out something about him in the 1851 Census of Marnoch. The stone was erected by William McBain, who was thirty-four years old, was a farmer, and had a wife, Betsy (32), and two sons, John (6) and James (1). Living with them at that time was a visitor, Janet Thomson.

The name Fill the Cap could also be seen on a stone in the row of tombstones behind the Bain grave. This was the burial place of Mary S. McHardie, who 'died at Fill the Cap, Marnoch, April 1875, aged 40 years,' and also of John McRobert, who died at Fill the Cap in February 1885, aged 60 years. Also on the stone were the names of Mary Jane McRobert, who died at Mosshead, Kinnairdy, and Alexander McRobert, who died at Aberchirder.

So where was Fill the Cap? And what did the name mean? Despite help from libraries, talking to local people, and studying old maps and documnts, I found it difficult to get any answers to these questions, But there was one possible clue. In the 1851 Census there were four tenants at Fill the Cap – a total of thirteen people. The heads of the households were William McBain, Peter McArthur, a Chelsea pensioner, George Christie, a tinsmith, and James Innes, a mole catcher. In other words, Fill the Cap was one of the old farm 'touns.'

There were five other 'touns' in the Census list for Marnoch – Jeanfield, (eight people), Forgiestown (fourteen people), Dundee (four people), Dubieton (nine people), and Howmoss (six people). All these ferm touns were given in a list of Marnoch place names except one, Fill the Cap, and all five appear in up-to-date Ordnance Survey maps, grouped together east of Kinnairdy Castle. It was then that David Catto, Local Studies Librarian with the Aberdeenshire Council, sent me copies of two old maps, one dated 1877, the other 1905. Both of them showed Fill the Cap, marked down in tiny lettering, *Fillthecap*, between two of the 'touns' on the census list: Janefield Croft and Fergustown.

From Marnoch I drove past Kinnairdy Castle, whose slender tower rose high above the Deveron, and at Dubietown (given in OS maps as Dubiton) I turned up a narrow side road to Forgieston. Beyond it was

Kinnairdy Castle.

The deserted Fill-the-Cap cottar house.

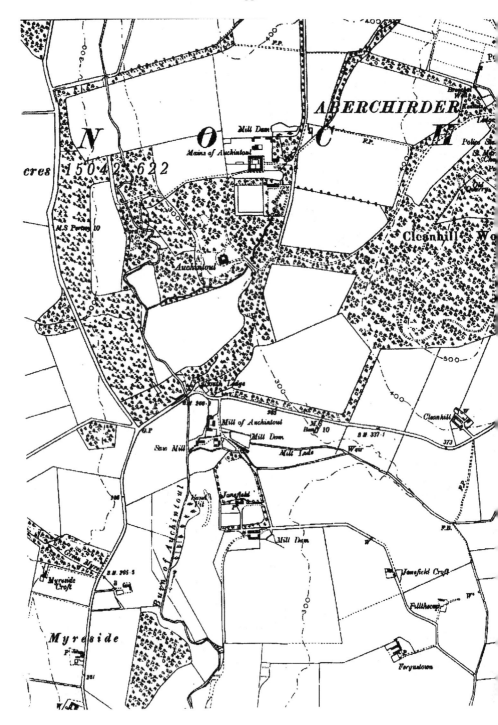

An old map showing 'Fi[...]

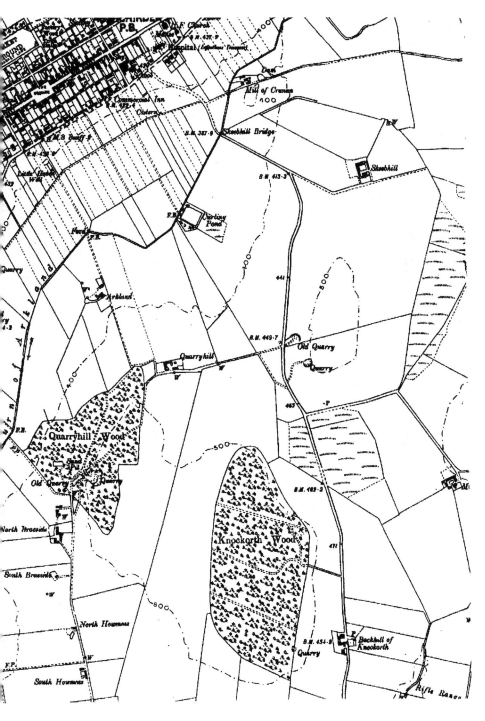

’ near Kinnairdy Castle.

Janefield and as I drove towards it I saw a deserted cottar house in the middle of a field on my right. That, I thought, was Fill-the-Cap – or what was left of it.

I wanted to confirm that it was Fill-the-Cap, so I went on to Janefield, where Margaret Wilson and her brother James have lived since 1945. They confirmed that the cottar house was Fill-the-Cap, but had no idea what the name meant. When they moved into Janefield there was a tenant in the cottar house, which was let out by the people at Forgieston. I went back up the road and tramped through the field to take a closer look at it. There was a huge space where there had been a door, which suggested that Fill-the-Cap had been a but-and-ben, with part of it housing his beasts.. There was a big open fireplace at the other end and the roof had timber lining. Outside, a holly tree and an elder clung together.

So that was Fill-the-Cap. I had seen it, but I still didn't know what the name meant. I knew what Janefield meant. Margaret Wilson told me it hadn't always been a farmhouse and that the Jane who gave it her name was a Jane Innes. This was Innes country. I was to discover later that there were Fill-the-Caps in Banff. The *Annals of Banff* carried a reference to Lord Fife's 'dyke of Fillacap' and Lady Gight was said to have a house called Little Fillacap. There was even a Muckle-fill-the Caup (note the spelling). This was the name of a site on which the ruinous Church of St Mary's stood. Later, I was to track down Fill-the-Caps in sixteenth century Aberdeen. But I still had to find the meaning of the name . . .

22

ABERDOUR HOUSE

The wild, stormy coast of Aberdour, the most northerly parish of Aberdeenshire, has held a long-lasting fascination for me. It was where the Pictish saint St Drostan landed from Caithness on his way to Christianise Buchan and eventually to found the Monastery of Deer. It was where one of the planned villages of Buchan was laid out by William Gordon in 1798, its parallel streets sloping down to the sea. It has been described as 'romantic', with tumbling streams dropping down deep ravines that cleave the high ground, but it can be savage and unfriendly.

The New Aberdour coastline is pockmarked with caves, among them the Cat's Hole or Cat's Eye and the Ceard's Cove, where tinkers once made their homes. There is a spot near here where a tinker woman commited suicide, throwing herself from a huge rock that became known as the Auld Wife's Loup. Then there is the Hermit's Cave, where a retired sea captain lived, and the Reid Coo's Haven, and the Cave of Cowhaven, where Lord Pitsligo hid from the Hanoverians in the winter of 1746–7. His cave was said to 'run up into the country nobody knows how far'.

Up above Cullykhan Bay, beyond Pennan, there is a great gash in the land known as Hell's Lum. The Devil must have stretched his horny hand over neighbouring Aberdour, for there was 'wickedness and witchcraft' there in the old days. In 1701 the kirk session was so disturbed by 'the great abounding of uncleanness' in the parish that it ordered a 'four-nooked big stool' to be made. It had to be an ell high and placed before the pulpit 'to be a terror to faulters'.

Andrew Cumine made the faulters' stool from an old broken boat and was paid five shillings for it. Six months later, George Michie and his wife Helen Lamb, from Quarryhead, were hauled before the session for resorting to charms to heal their sick child. They were told by a beggar wife to lay hot stones above the door, which they did, but the thatch caught fire and their house, barns and byres were 'burnt to ashes'.

It was, said the session, the just judgement of God and it was decided to deal with the couple 'on the next Lord's Day'. They duly turned up at the kirk, the four-nooked stool was taken out, and they were 'publikly rebuked for their charming'. Whether or not it proved to be a terror to these poor people is not recorded.

When I learned that my mother, Lizzie Murdoch, worked and lived in Aberdour, I sometimes wondered if I was walking in her footsteps when I began exploring the area. She must have known the names of many of the farms scattered along this rocky coast – Poukburn (the stream is called 'the Pouk'); Quarryhead, which the native tongue has turned into Coral Heid, just as it has turned Ironhill into Eernel; Happyhillock and Pittendrum. Pittendrum, which is said to mean 'ridge-town,' is near Sandhaven. It was Pittendrum that supplied the first half of a rhyme containing some curious weather lore. It told you what happened when the waves came rumbling in over the pebbly shore. 'Fin the rumble comes fae Pittendrum,' it said, 'the ill weather's a' tae cum.' Local folk told me it was usually correct.

Young Lizzie could never have foreseen that one day her son would be wandering about Aberdour searching for the meaning of all these queer names. It is almost certain that one of her walks would have taken her down the rough road to the sea, where the second half of the weather rhyme was completed – 'Fin the rumble comes fae Aberdour,' it said, 'the ill weather's a' ower.'

The author Catherine Gavin wrote about the shore road 'falling away from the modern world.' I could understand what she meant, but there is a car park there now and the modern world has come back again, this time with cars and litter and vandalism. It was there that I met Charlie Morrison, from Huntly, who has been there for thirty years. 'I'm just an incomer,' he said. He works at the Mill Farm and had come down to the bay to see the vandalism that had been done overnight to a wooden barrier marking the parking area. Charlie has been around, working at various places, and he knew Marnoch – he had relatives there.

He told me that a new man from abroad had taken over Aberdour

Aberdour House.

House and was 'doing it all up'. I had seen only a photograph of the house and I remembered being surprised by the number of windows on the front of it. There were twenty windows – twenty-three if you threw in skylights on the roof. There have been a number of notable mansions in this part of the North-east, not least among them being the palace of the Bairds of Auchmedden, demolished in the late 18th century, and Old Troup House, built in 1760 and replaced in 1897 by, as Charles McKean put it in his *Illustrated Architectural Guide*, 'the current Baronial confection by R. G. Wilson.' Photographs of Old Troup House show it as a clone of Aberdour House, with twenty windows in the front, and no skylights, but I could count another nine on the gable-end. What did they do with all those windows?

The House of Aberdour was built in 1746 by Samuel Forbes of Skellater and was at one time a lairdship of the Gordons. It is a plain, unpretensious building, three storeys high and built to withstand the storms that come skirling off the fretful sea. The land here is owned by John Fowlie, a neighbouring farmer, who bought Aberdour House some years ago and later sold it. There were other buyers before the present occupant, Robin Mackinlay, took it over.

When you approach the entrance a weather cock can be seen rising above one of the farm outbuildings. It tops an unusual square, pyramid-roofed doocot, which looks down on a quadrangular steading dating back to 1740. The steading was at one time completely covered in, but it had to be taken down. The doocot must claim a high place in the doocot ratings, but the roof below it is badly in need of repair and there has been word that it may have to be demolished. That would be a pity – let's hope it can be saved.

As Charles McKean wrote in his architectural guide, this old Scots house has 'little fashionable pretension,' but behind its sombre frontage is a house of considerable charm and character. You walk through endless corridors, pass through countless doors, peer into the past, marvel at the staircase and elegant lounge, and listen nervously for the sound of ghostly footsteps. No decent mansion house is complete without its ghost, and Aberdour was said to have one.

Robin Mackinlay and his wife Elizabeth took over the house six years

The pyramid-roofed doocot at Aberdour House,
looking down in a quadrangle steading dating back to 1740.

The entrance to Aberdour House.

ago and are gradually adapting it to their own thinking. Robin worked in the Far East for twenty-six years. His wife is Welsh and likes living in Aberdour – she thinks the countryside is like home. When they moved into the house a window cleaner asked her how many windows there were. She said she didn't know, but she would count them. There are sixty-three.

Robin took me all round the house, over its three storeys. You could get lost in it. There are sixteen rooms on the ground floor. Originally, you had to walk through each room to get from one to the other, but a corridor was added and now you enter by a door in the corridor. Elizabeth spoke about the 'Victorianisation' of the house. The Victorian occupants had left their mark on the building; they had transformed it, changing the staircase, for instance, and making the house warmer.

There had been two kitchens, one with a big open fireplace. I could imagine the pots and kettles and swey that once hung over it, and there was some discussion about whether this was where the farm servants were fed or whether it had been a chaumer, a sleeping place for farm workers. I was taken up a short but steep flight of stairs into the loft, where the servants were said to be accommodated. If this low-roofed, gloomy area was where my mother had slept when she was a servant at Aberdour it was certainly nothing to write home about. It was more likely to be where the Aberdour ghost hung out.

Elizabeth Mackinlay told me about the spectre. Various things had gone missing, and a painter working in the house told her he had put her shoes up to her room. He had found them sitting on a step pointing into the house. Later, a local woman told her that there *was* a ghost. She had seen her walking along the drive to the house – the white lady.

I was, however, less interested in the ghosts who had flitted along the corridors of the old house than I was in the real-life lairds, for, when we were talking about previous owners I found that I had another link with Aberdour. This happened when Robin was showing me a cutting, dated May 1934, which said that the Aberdeenshire estate of Aberdour, including the village lands and superiority of New Aberdour, belonging to Mr A. Dingwall Fordyce of Brucklay had been sold.

The names Brucklay and Dingwall Fordyce struck an immediate bell with me, for I had an uncle who had been grieve at Shevado, the Home Farm on the Brucklay estate. His name was Alec Murdoch – and his sister was my mother, Lizzie Murdoch. Whether or not it was mere coincidence that they both worked for the Fordyce family at Aberdour *and* Brucklay I never discovered.

The Aberdour estate was bought by John Duff Dingwall of Brucklay from William Gordon in 1923, but it was the Brucklay factor who moved into Aberdour House, not John Dingwall. He stayed at Brucklay. There were other properties involved in that deal, for Rosehearty and Pennan were also swept into the Brucklay net. The ruined castle of Dundargue, once a stronghold of the Comyns, and captured in 1333 from an Englishman, Henry de Beaumont, by the Earl of Moray, also came into the possession of the Dingwall-Fordyce family.

Elizabeth Mackinlay told me that when workmen were painting the house after they moved in she had seen at the bottom of one wall the names of the men who had painted it in 1923. The words 'Old Deer' were also on the wall, which made it obvious that estate workers from Brucklay had been sent to Aberdour to do the job. The Brucklay family had enough money to buy the estate, but in the end it boomeranged on them. Although they owned the estate for quite a long time they had no money to do much with it.

In the years before the war I spent many a holiday at Shevado. I remember riding up to Brucklay Castle with my Uncle Alec in a truck carrying a huge block of ice for the pantry. Heavy rates and repair bills brought about a decision to take its roof off in 1951. Brucklay had been in the hands of the Dingwall-Fordyce family since 1744, when the estates of Culsh and Brucklay were merged. 'Heaven's in the wid o' Brucklay' went the lines of an old song, and for me it was true. Many years later, when I was writing about Buchan, I climbed a steeple-like tower built on the Hill of Culsh in memory of Dingwall Fordyce, MP.

Now, into the twenty-first century, Aberdour and Brucklay face contrasting fortunes. Robin and Elizabeth Mackinlay bring a new lease of life to the old house with sixty-three windows. Brucklay, on the other hand, was put up for sale in twenty separate lots. Brucklay's ruined sixteenth-century castle was one lot, and there were others that held sentimental memories for me, among them the steading, where as a loon I nibbled at cattle food in a loft above the joiner's shop, and the Shevado

Ruined Brucklay Castle, once the home of the Laird of Aberdour.

farmhouse, where I lay in an upstairs bedroom in my uncle's cottage and listened to the melancholy whistle of a train disappearing down the Buchan line.

When I left Aberdour House I made for the village and the shore road. Down there was the old kirkton of Aberdour, or what was left of it, and its ruined church, perched on a shelf above the ravine of the Dour burn. There is an unusual square doocot built into one of the kirk's dykes. The kirkyard groans under the weight of ancient stones, many flat on their backs, their lichen-covered lettering almost impossible to read. There are burial-aisles for various lairds' families, the Leslies of Coburty and the Bairds of Auchmedden.

Down there, too, is St Drostan's Well, which was erected in 1884 on a

This striking steeple-like tower stands on the Hill of Culsh
at Strichen, built in 1515 by the tenants of Brucklay estate
in memory of William Dingwall-Fordyce, M.P. There is a
spiral staircase in the tower and from the high level a
breathtaking view of the Buchan landscape unfolds.
The name Culsh comes from *cuillie*, a 'corner' or 'recess'.

natural spring, said to be the spot where St Drostan landed. The *Book of Deer* recorded how Columba and his pupil Drostan came to Aberdour: 'With Drostam his pupil he came from Hi (Iona) as God had shown him, unto Abbordoboir, and Bede the Cruithnach (Pict) was Mormaor of Buchan before him; and it was he that gave them that *cathair* (town) in freedom for ever from Moirmaor and Toisach.'

I left Aberdour when the sun was beginning to sink, putting a soft glow on a tranquil sea. I was thinking then of the old story of how Columba accompanied Drostan to Deer and saw him settled before returning to Iona. When they parted 'their tears flowed' and Columba said, 'Let this place be *Deara* (Gaelic: tears) from henceforth.' Today, people put their packs on their backs and set out on a kind of latter-day pilgrimage along the roads that Drostan took from Aberdour to Deer. This was the route that beckoned me.

23

BOOK OF DEER

Old Deer is a small, sleepy Buchan village on the banks of the Ugie. It lives up to its name, for it has an old, venerable look about it. It was in this corner of the North-east that St Drostan founded the Celtic monastery of Deer. The monastery was built on or near the site of the present parish church, and it was there that the famous *Book of Deer* was written between the ninth and twelfth centuries.

I was thinking of Dr John Pratt when I walked down the main street of the village, for he was born at the Slacks of Cairnbanno, New Deer, and became curate at Old Deer when it merged with Stuartfield. He was my guide, taking me through what he called 'this village of great antiquity,' describing it as it was thirty years before he wrote his classic book, *Buchan*, in 1858. Like most old villages, he said, it was 'a mean unsightly place, consisting of one street, but separated into two branches at the kirk-style (the gate of the churchyard), most of the houses being built with the gable end to the street.'

Going down the brae, treading in his footsteps, I was heading for two kirks that had dominated that 'mean unsightly place' nearly two centuries ago, and which still do today. Deer Parish Church and the Episcopal Church of St Drostan stand only a stone's throw from each other, as if in some saintly communion, but in 1711 their congregations were at each other's throats over a bid by the Presbyterians to replace an Episcopalian minister with one of their own.

Deer Parish Church, with its tall, slim tower and pyramid spire, first claims your attention, but St Drostan's, sitting back snugly from the street, has a solid Buchan look about it. I have often thought that Buchan builds its kirks like fortresses, with soaring spires and solid granite walls to keep Auld Nick out. Dr Pratt pondered on 'how far the feeling, not to say the principle, of *symbolism* is traceable in these older parish churches.' He thought that they certainly seemed to harmonise much more closely with the peculiarities of the Presbyterian form of worship.

Dr Pratt said that the style of the Old Deer Parish Church was common to the period – plain and substantial, but with no particular architectural character. Nevertheless, it was built for great things, for the *Statistical Account* said it was 'fitted up to contain 1,200 sitters', a figure hard to swallow when kirks today are emptying like deflated balloons. So large a congregation for so small a place. Yet nothing is surprising in this tiny village and you may even come to believe the curious legend that hangs over the parish church. It is said that when various sites were chosen for the new church a voice was heard crying:

'It is not here, it is not here
That ye're to big the Kirk o' Deer,
But on the tap o' Tillery,
Where many a corpse shall lie.

Old Deer Parish Church.

Whether or not the clerics paid heed to some ghostly voice giving them their building instructions, the Kirk o' Deer was certainly 'biggit' on a knoll known as Tap Tillery, within a bend of the South Ugie. Ground was set aside for a burial place on the assumption that the 'weird', or prophecy, would come true, which it did. But if you really want to know what put Old Deer on the map you will find the answer on a small wall panel near the entrance to the church. It reads: 'In the Celtic monastery in this vicinity was written the Book of Deer, which includes the oldest known examples of Scottish Gaelic.'

This valuable document was lost for centuries. It was discovered in 1857 among a number of neglected books in Cambridge University Library. It is still there, a very small book, bound in skin. It contains the complete Gospel of St John and portions of other three gospels in Latin, transcribed in about AD 700. On the margins of the manuscript are added *notitia* in Gaelic of the eleventh or twelfth centuries, jottings of priceless value as a source of information about Celtic Scotland. The pages are ruled with a sharp pointed instrument and the letters placed under the lines, not on them.

Old Deer, smaller than New Deer, has always basked in the glory of the *Book of Deer*. It has always been considered the 'capital' of the area, probably because up until the second half of the eighteenth century it was the main populated place, not only in the parish, but in the whole valley of the South Ugie. Now there are six villages, four of them founded by James Ferguson of Pitfour.

There is no trace left of the monastery where the monks worked on the *Book of Deer,* but about three-quarters of a mile west of where it stood is the Cistercian abbey that succeeded it in 1218. It was founded by William Comyn, Earl of Buchan, built in a lonely waste of marsh and forest, sheltered from the north by Saplin Brae. By all accounts, monastic life in the abbey had its ups and downs. In 1537 a special commission was set up to deal with complaints by the monks, bearing in mind 'the difficult situation of the place, and the malignity of the time.' They laid down 'fixed sums of money and victuals for the honourable maintenance in food, clothing and are necessaries of the brothers.'

The 'necessaries' included a loaf of good flour each day, along with two cakes or loaves of oatmeal. A pound of pepper a year was given, and for the butter of the whole convent forty shillings yearly, also eight dozen poultry, and in Lent forty salmon, with salt in sufficient quantity for the cook's table, and for the seasoning of the flesh and fish of the convent. Two oxen

Abbey of Deer ruins

were purchased annually about Easter and these were fattened along with others for the convent and for the guests' table. They were also allowed thirty lambs a year.

The abbey fell into disrepair after the Reformation. The man behind its downfall was the last of the commendator abbots, Robert Keith, second son of the Earl Marischal, and a man who was said to be 'a sordid and double-minded person'. He gained control of the abbey funds and turned the property into a temporal lordship of Altrie. His aim was 'the dissolution of the Abbacy of Deir from the state and condition of a Monastery thereof into a temporal lordship'. With the transfer of all power and rights to the kindred of the Earl Marischal the religious work of the Abbey came to an end.

Over the years the abbey was left to decay. At one point it became a quarry for building materials. In 1809, James Ferguson of Pitfour (1734–1820) was concerned about the state of the abbey buildings. Ferguson was an extraordinary man. He drove turnpike roads through Buchan, countered the 'treeless Buchan' jibe by planting miles of hawthorn hedges, laid out great plantations on his own estate at Pitfour, built a lake of forty-five acres, and adorned it with a miniature facsimile of the Temple of Theseus in Athens. Troubled by what was happening to the abbey, he tidied up the site and also did a certain amount of rebuilding, but it was all in vain. Everything changed when his kinsman Admiral George Ferguson took over the estate in 1854.

They called him the Mad Admiral. He built a racecourse – the Ascot of Buchan – erected an Observatory from which he could watch the races (it is still there today), held gambling parties at Pitfour that were the talk of the neighbourhood, and had an army of servants to look after his needs. The Pitfour fortunes slipped away. This eccentric laird plundered what was left of the abbey, levelling the remains of the abbey church to build a family mausoleum. The mausoleum was later demolished and since 1930 the ruins have been under government care.

There has been a slow revival of interest in the *Book of Deer*, bringing about the setting up of a *Book of Deer* project, but it is unlikely to reach the heights it did in the eighteenth and nineteenth centuries, when two Buchan clubs were formed to guard the interests of this remarkable document. The Old Deer Club was founded in 1792 and continued until 1837, while the Club of Deer came into being in 1868 and lasted until 1902.

There was also what Alexander Keith described in his book, *A Thousand Years of Aberdeen*, as 'a remarkable society that called itself the Academy of Deer.' 'This company,' he wrote, 'was wont to meet in the manse of Old Deer in Buchan, the incumbent, the Rev. James Peter, acting as chairman and host with the title of Abbot.' James Peter, 'lover of good talk, good books, good art, good wine, and good company,' was also largely responsible for the resuscitation of the Club of Deer.

Keith wrote in a footnote: 'The occasion for the resuscitation was the sale of a deceased Church of Scotland minister's effects, which included some excellent claret purchased by the clerical brethren and sampled at a lunch convened on the spot. At the time of writing (1972) the club has celebrated with full appropriate pomp and circumstance, the centenary of its second founding.'

In 1896 a new book of Deer made an appearance, but this one had a different title – *Book of the Parish of Deir*. Note the old-style spelling. It was issued in connection with a parish church bazaar, but its 104 pages had little resemblance to the type of material normally found in other bazaar books. There was nothing light or frivolous about it – not even a single poem. It dealt with historical aspects of the parish and the editor, the Rev. Alexander Lawson, who later became Professor of English Literature at St Andrews University, provided no fewer than six papers. They included

'The Parish, Its Name and Limits', 'The Abbey of Deir', 'The Parish and Ministers of Deir', and 'The Book of Deir'.

Professor Cooper of Glasgow, then minister of the East Church, Aberdeen, dealt with the patron saint St Drostan and another contributor was James Ferguson of Kinmundy, later proprietor of Pitfour estate. He laid emphasis on Old Deer enjoying a distinction which made it unique among the parishes of Scotland – 'to it belongs the honour of being the centre from which Christianity was first preached in the Northern Lowlands, and the credit of having made and kept for centuries the oldest Scottish book.'

The year 1910 saw the publication by the Buchan Club of *The Book of Buchan*, edited by J. F. Tocher. James Fowler Tocher was the Aberdeenshire county analyst and a member of an exclusive club called 'The Sit Siccars', whose members were close friends of Charles ('Hamewith') Murray. Murray wrote a poem entitled 'J.F.T.':

He's just a livin' 'Wha is Wha',
Kens Dukes an' Earls an' Lords o' Law,
Provosts an' Lairds, an' wi' them a'
He mixes level.

The *Book of Buchan* carried an article by Tocher on the *Book of Deer,* and a piece by Professor Andrew Lawson on the Abbey of Deer. Tocher said that the *Book of Deer* was not only full of interest, but it was also very valuable and, he added, 'somewhat puzzling to the philologist'. Names of places which frequently appeared in the book were extremely difficult to identify with modern sites, although many attempts had been made to trace their origin and meaning. Some were easily identified, but others like Dabaei, Durchat, and Pet Ipuir were fanciful and unsound.

William Alexander said in his *Place-Names of Aberdeenshire* that there were some thirty places in Buchan mentioned in the *Book of Deer,* but only a few were identifiable with certainty. There was no doubt about names like Aberdober (Aberdour), Turbruaid (Turriff) and Helain (Ellon) and there were some that were fairly certain, such as Alteri (Altrie) and Elerc (Elrick) and Auchad Madchor (Auchmachar). There was also Bibin, which was Biffie. Old Deer was known as Biffie, a name that I first heard in an old *rhyme*:

At Saplin Brae
I brak' my tae;
I shod my horse at Biffie.

Alexander's verdict on the book was that it was 'a document that raised more questions than answers.' He was probably right, but to the place-name addict there is an irresistible challenge in trying to make sense of these ancient names.

The *Book of Buchan* published charters, some during the late sixteenth century, which shed light on the relinquishing of abbey lands to Robert Keith and the Earl Marischal. Keith's intentions were abundantly clear. The abbey, he said, had been 'of auld erectit and foundit' and was now to be 'alluterlie abolischeit, sua that na memorie thaireof sall be heirafter.'

Some of the names in the charters are familiar, but with unfamiliar spelling: Auchrdie, Auchmwygel, Quartaillhouse, Carnebannock, Glauckriach, Rippieraw and Parkhouse of Biffie, Monkiehill, Bruehill and the Kerktown if Deir. To take just one, Glauckriach is Clackriach in Old Deer. It comes from *glac riabhach,* 'the grey-coloured ravine'. The castle of Clackriach stood in the ravine.

Today, the Abbey of Deer is an oasis in the rush and bustle of busy Buchan. Traffic roars west to some of James Ferguson's 'new' villages, but walk into the pillared entrance to the abbey grounds and you are in another world. No commendators to trouble you. No mad admirals to plunder what is left of the shattered abbey. You can walk through the ruins and try to pick out the monks' dormitory, or the cellars with the kitchen in the western section, or the refectory where the brothers dined in silence, nibbling away at their loaves of bread.

Meanwhile, a group of dedicated people are thinking of the first monastery in Old Deer, where the *Book of Deer* was written. The Central Tourism Group founded the Book of Deer Project with the aim of raising the awareness of the historic document. There was a close working link with Aberdeen University and the Elphinstone Institute and Aberdeenshire Council gave their support too. The project now has a Book of Deer Centre in Aden Park. I went there with George Smart, chairman of the project. He told me he had fifty-three friends of the project and was always looking for more.

Inside the centre the walls are covered with blown-up pages of the *Book of Deer* and in one corner there is a copy of it made to actual size. It seemed a tiny book to have so much history on its shoulders. Looking at it, I thought that the *real* Book of Deer should be in Aberdeen University, or the Elphinstone Institute, and not in Cambridge. Back in 1927, George Fraser, Aberdeen's librarian, told how Cambridge University Library cared for it 'as one of the most precious documents in that great collection'.

George Smart, chairman of the Book of Deer Project, with a copy of the
Book of Deer.

'Not very long ago,' he said, 'I was taken by the Cambridge University librarian to see it. He took me to a special glass case, always kept covered, and when he lifted out the precious volume – which has the glass case to itself – and placed it in my hands, I suggested that as it really belonged to Aberdeenshire it should be returned to the Public Library or the University Library of Aberdeen. He smiled very nicely, but he would not make any promise.'

That was more than seventy years ago. Perhaps it is time that someone reminded the Cambridge authorities that the *Book of Deer* should be sent home.

24

UNCLE TAMMIE

Walter Gregor was well known for his work on North-east folklore and place names, but there were other unusual interests that he tried to develop – folk-riddles and counting-out rhymes. In 1887, writing in the publication *Scottish Notes and Queries,* he said that it was time to gather riddles that still existed because, before many years had passed, they would be lost.

He asked his readers to send in specimens and in the July edition of *SN&Q* he printed a few from the North-east.

LONMAY

Two men's length
Two men's strength,
Two men cudna tear it,
But a little boy can carry it.

A Rope.

ABERDOUR

What is't that's nae and never 'll be?
Haud up her han', an that ye'l see.

The fingers all the same length.

RATHEN

As I gaed ower the Brig o' Dee
I met Uncle Tammie,

Wi'a'the wardle on's back –
Wasna he a clever mannie?
The Mole.

England exported the art of riddling to Scotland. It was popular with adults until about the seventeenth century, when it became a children's game. One of the first books of riddles printed in England was called *Demandes Joyous*. It was printed in 1511 by Caxton's apprentice, Wynkyn de Worde.

Rhyming riddles were all the vogue in Elizabethan England. They usually described everyday objects, such as this one:

Little Nancy Etticoat,
With a white petticoat.
And a red nose;
She has no feet or hands,
The longer she stands,
The shorter she grows.
A lighted candle.

So how far back do riddles go? Walter Gregor gave a Biblical riddle about a hunter and his prey which was said to have appeared in the work of a learned Greek, Michael Constantinus Psellus, of Constantinople, born about 1020 AD. 'Some, like the Sphinx riddle, and the one that is said to have caused the death of Homer, are very old, and widely spread,' wrote Gregor. 'Some appear in almost very language in Europe, e.g., the coffin and egg riddles.'

Gregor said that the subject of folk-riddles was full of interest, and, like most other subjects of folk-lore, raised many questions still awaiting a full solution. 'I hope I have said enough to call forth many workers,' he added.

Despite his appeal no more riddles appeared in *Scottish Notes and Queries*. Nevertheless, the North-east has produced a large number of its own local riddles over the years. Oddly enough, one of them was an egg riddle:

There's a wee house in the hill
Wi' neither door or window in't,
An' yet there's men's meat in't.
An egg.

As I gaed to my father's feast
I met an alazouzous beast,
Ten heads, ten tails.

Forty feet, fower score nails.
  A sow with a litter of pigs.

Four upstanders, four dirry daners,
Two turn-abouts and a waggle.
  A cow's legs, paps, ears, tail.

Hairy oot, hairy in,
A'hair an' nae skin.
  A hair rope.

As I gaed ower the Brig o' Dee
I met a Latin scholar,
And drew off his hat,
And drew off his glove,
Now tell me the name of that scholar.
  Andrew

As I went ower the Brig o' Dee
I met George Macquahan,
I took off his head and drunk his blood
And left his body stan'in.
  A bottle of ale.

Gregor wrote about counting-out rhymes at the end of the nineteenth century, but counting out was still in vogue up to the last war. When children played games like Hide and Seek, counting out was used to determine who would be the chaser. One youngster recited a rhyme while pointing out the others one by one. When the rhyme ended the last to be pointed out became the chaser.

Gregor described counting out as 'a curious item of folk-lore, common among different nations in a variety of forms.' He gave a number of counting-out rhymes from Banffshire and Aberdeenshire:

As I gaed up the aipple tree,
A'the aipples stack t'me,
Fite puddin, black trout,
I choose you oot,
For a dirty dish clout.

Counting out was often done with a nonsense rhyme and frequently ended with the phrase 'Stan' ye oot by!'. Fraserburgh was well to the forefront with rhymes like these:

Eetum, peetum, penny pump,
Cock-a-leerie, jinky gye,
Stan' ye oot by
For a bonny penny pie.

or

Eetum, peetum, penny pump,
A' the laadies in a lump;
Sax or saiven in a clew,
A' made wi candy glue.

Ink, pink,
Penny, stink.

One, two, three, four,
Tack a mell an ding 'im ower.

One, two three, four, five six, siven,
A' that fisher dodds widna win t' heaven.

Eerinnges, oranges, two for a penny,
A'm a good scholar for coontin so many.

Time has 'coontit oot' the stories that lay behind these jingles. Who, for instance, was John Hamilton, who featured in a rhyme from Tyrie?

Eetum for peetum,
The King cam' t' meet him,
And dang John Hamilton doon.

There was another John, an Englishman, who featured in a rhyme from Portsoy:

Enerie, twaarie, ackterie, ten,
Allabie, crackabie, ten, or eleevin,
Pim, pam, musky dam,
Queevrie,Quaavrie, English man.

And there was Mary from Portsoy:

Eerie, aarie,
Biscuit Mary,
Pim, pam, pot.

Biscuit Mary, who featured in one of Walter Gregor's
riddles, came from Portsoy, probably from a
back street like the one pictured above.

There were no Aberdeen rhymes in Gregor's list, but I remember two
which were chanted in the streets of the city when I was a loon. One was
the brief, 'Eetle, ottle, black bottle, eetle ottle out.' The other began 'Eenie,
meenie, miny mo . . .' which was said to be the most popular rhyme in this
country and in America. Whether or not the remaining lines were
Aberdeen's own version I never discovered, but this is how it went:

Eeenie, meenie, miny mo,
Sit the baby on the po',
When its done wipe its bum,
An' shove the paper up the lum.

25

MOUNTHOOLY

It was the fourth of July – Independence Day. The year was 1945, and I was standing on the steps of John Knox Church, Mounthooly, in Aberdeen, newly married and musing on the fact that I had just lost *my* independence. I had come home on leave from the R.A.F. to be married, having unromantically proposed to my wife-to-be on a No. 1 Bridge of Don tramcar rattling down King Street. She said 'Yes!' as we pitched round the Castlegate corner into Union Street.

The Mounthooly church was my wife's kirk. This was alien territory to me, coming as I did from a tenement in Rosemount, half-way across the town, but I came to know it well in the post-war years. The wedding reception was a wartime lunch in the Northern Hotel. Unfortunately, the photographer had a liquid lunch and failed to turn up, so we had pictures taken in my mother-in-law's 'backie' against a line of washing.

I went back to John Knox Church recently and stood on those steps again. I was looking at a different picture from the one I had seen more than half a century ago. Now, the streets had changed, houses had vanished, shops had disappeared, and cars roared round a monstrous traffic roundabout, which some people called Aberdeen's Piccadilly Circus.

The 'Bobbies' Boxie', a police sub-station, had gone, as had the tenement next to it, Nos. 6-10, which had Walter Michie's grocer's shop on the ground floor. The properties of Joseph Carcone had vanished and no longer could you sniff the air for the scrumptious smell of Bendelow's pies.

Mounthooly Church.

No more mince pies. No more apple bannocks. They were 'as tasty as kitchie, het, sappy and fine', but they belonged to a more sensitive past.

I have often wondered how Mounthooly got its name. It somehow or other never seemed to fit the area. Even G.M. Fraser, the city librarian, who was a walking encyclopaedia when it came to Aberdeen street names, was stumped by Mounthooly. 'I mean Mounthooly!' he said contemptuously. 'Since the middle of the eighteenth century the name has been variously spelt Mount Hooley, Mount Heillie, Mountheely, Mount Hillie; and again Mount Hooley, but there is no special significance in that.'

The name wasn't a local one, confined to Aberdeen. There was a positive plague of Mounthoolys. They could be found in Roxburghshire, Linlithgowshire, in Buchan (near Pitsligo), and in Peterhead, where a street known as James Street was formerly Mounthooly. There was one in Wick, another at Kirk, where a chapel stood, and one in Dunnet. There was also a Mounthooly Lane in Kirkwall.

Fraser thought 'hoolie' or 'hillie' might be a pleonasm, which sent me scurrying to the dictionary. It seems that a pleonasm is 'an expression in which certain words are redundant, as in a false untruth.' In the end, however, he was convinced that the 'halie', 'holy', or 'heilie' was simply the ordinary spelling in use in the Middle centuries for 'holy', and that the name was the Holy Mount, meaning that it was church land, or that a church or chapel stood there.

He backed this up by drawing attention to a piece of land in the Spital known as the 'holylande'. It went back to 1492, when Andrew Ancroft, a burgess of Aberdeen, 'sold an annual rent of twenty shillings to Mr Symon Dods, said rents to be drawn from his two crofts of land lying on the north side of the town – one of which was 'the penny croft, and my other croft or land extending from the top of the hill downwards to the holylande'.

So much for Mounthooly. My attention had now shifted to Mr Dods's rents, which were coming from two crofts north of the town, one of them a penny croft. I had already become interested in the crofts that were once scattered in and around Aberdeen and my curiosity was increased when I found that there was a Mounthooly Croft near John Knox Church, where I had been married. According to Fraser, it formed one of the zone of crofts of land within the town's inner marches.

It was in this area that a Leper House, or Sick House, was set up when the dreaded disease of leprosy struck Aberdeen towards the end of the sixteenth century. William Kennedy, in his *Annals of Aberdeen*, wrote about how the virulence and terror of the disease divided families: 'it not unfrequently occasioned the husband to forsake his wife, and the wife and children to abandon the husband and the father, while the unhappy patient was interdicted from holding intercourse with the brewer, the baker, or the butcher.'

The Sick House lay between the Gallow-hill and the Spital road, a little north of the Mounthooly Croft, while beyond it were the Lepers Croft and the Lepers Myre. In the earliest historical register of Aberdeen, kept by Walter Cullen, Reader in St Nicholas Church, it was said that in 1590 'ane lepar boy in ye lepar howss of Aberdene departitt (this life) ye 27th October.' In 1592 an Act was passed laying down that the Leper House would be entitled to one peat from every load put up for sale in Aberdeen and in Old Aberdeen. By the seventeenth century the Leper House was virtually in disuse and in 1604 the kirk session of St Nicholas gave over the keys to Helene Smyth, 'ane puir woman infectit with Leprosie'. By 1661 it was all over and the Leper House was in ruins.

The original settlement at Mounthooly is not shown in Parson Gordon's Plan of 1661, although it can be fairly accurately guessed at by relating it to the Gallowgate head. In 1746, 'Mountholy' appeared in G. &

W. Paterson's Survey of Old and New Aberdeen, lying just north of Gallowgate head, and a later Plan of 1773 showed it as 'Mount Hilie', now a fair-sized clachan. Interestingly, William M. Alexander gave 'Mount Heillie' among his Aberdeenshire place names, but he also mentioned the Aberdeen Mount. 'Its popular explanation as "Holy mount",' he said, 'is worthless'. So much for G.M. Frasers's theory back in 1911.

Mount Hilie, Mount Heillie, Mount Hooly – whatever the name, you would have had a wonderful bird's-eye view of it if you had climbed to the top of the old Porthill Factory – the Barracks they called it – where linen was manufactured in the late eighteenth century. It was a giant of a building, dominating everything around it. Edward Meldrum drew a sketch of it in his *Aberdeen of Old*. There were sixty windows on its frontage. Meldrum described it as a 'unique and interesting industrial building.' Built in 1750-2 it was demolished in 1960 to make way for residential development.

It is generally known that as well as the Barracks and the gallows there was a windmill on the Gallowgate at one time. It was built in 1602 and was happily whirling round when Parson Gordon was drawing up his plan. The Porthill or Gallowgate-hill, he said, was 'ordinerlie called the Windmill Hill, because of the wind milne situated upon the tope thereoff.' Plays were held on Windmillhill at one time. Just to make sure everybody got it right, Parson Gordon made two windy entries on his map – the 'Wynde Hill' and the 'Wynd mill Hill'.

There was also a Windy Wynd, near the Gallowgate, which took you to the junction with Lochside, later Loch Street, and continued along Spring Garden, but it was gobbled up by Spring Garden in 1897. It was the start of the 'Way to the Stocked Heade', which followed the old Skene Road up by what is now Maberly Street, Rosemount Place, Midstocket Road and the Lang Stracht, streets that I knew well as a youngster. I grew up in the 'Stocket Heade'. I was born in a tenement in Wallfield Place, a street that was built on the estate of Wallfield or Well-field.

One end of Wallfield Place opened on to Rosemount Place, the other end to the steep brae of Craigie Loanings. G.M. Fraser said that in the old days the street name was sometime spelt Craggy Loanings. He thought that some people might have difficulty in finding the crags (rocks) that seemed to give the street its name. There were garages there when I was a boy and the only loaning or lane I remember was a muddy track behind them.

It was only recently, when I was reading Fraser's book of street names, that I learned to my surprise that a Mister Crag had lived in this area – and he owned a croft there. It all had something to do with an attestation to be made regarding endowments, part of which came from a burgess, Alexander Crag. The attestation read:

> And from his (Alexander Craig's) own croft commonly called
> the Cragvele lying to the west of the said burgh, near the king's
> highway which leads to Rubbislaw, called the Loaning . . .
> thirteen shillings and fourpence.

'This was Crag's Loaning,' wrote Fraser, 'a name that in the kindly Aberdonian manner, fond of diminutives, would soon become Craggy's Loaning, and so the Craigie Loaning, a name which, having subsisted for five centuries and a half, will, we trust, be retained for many years to come. At least one attempt has been made to change the name; perhaps it is as well that its history should be better known as something of a safeguard in the future.' Nearly a century has passed since that was written and Craigie Loanings is still there and still with the same name. If, however, Mr Crag had been around he might have argued that it was high time it was changed back to what it should have been from the start – Crag's Loaning.

Across the town there was a scattering of crofts around Gallowgate-head. Umphra's Croft was one of a number involved in a charitable bequest called Hay's Mortification. This was the repayment by Sir Alexander Hay of a family debt, granting the burgh of Aberdeen feu duties and annual rents from various crofts for the upkeep of the Bridge of Balgownie, then known as the Bridge of Don. Kilcroft was a croft 'with Kyll barne, yards and taill adjacent'. A taill was a long narrow piece of land jutting out from a larger piece, especially from a croft. To the west were the Preaching Friars Croft, Tolquhoun Croft and the oddly-named Aedipingle Croft, while farther north were the Croft of the Altar of St Mary Magdalene and 'a croft callit ye Calsay Croft.'

The crofters who lived in the Inner Marches of the town in the late eighteenth century must have felt another kind of wind blowing through their communities – the wind of change. In 1795, an Act of Parliament was passed to provide turnpike roads for Aberdeenshire. No one could have foreseen then what it would mean to settlements like Causewayend – 'Cassie-end', a name that meant what it said, that this was where the cassies ended and the road became a muddy track. The turnpikes were to alter all that.

One of the routes to be tackled was the old 'Highway to Inverury' from

Cauewayend from the Mounthooly Roundabout.

Aberdeen. Charles Abercrombie, an Edinburgh surveyor responsible for mapping the turnpikes, saw no reason to change the existing route – up by Gallowgatehead and on to Kittybrewster, Kintore and Inverurie. The Inverurie trustees would have accepted this line had it not been for an Aberdeen merchant, J. Staats Forbes, and three lawyers, Hugh Hutcheoin, Andrew Jopp and William Burnett. They wanted the link with Aberdeen to be farther west, along the line of George Street and Tannery Lane.

The subscribers, who stood to gain from the rise in value of the land adjoining the new line of road, set out to convince other trustees of the wisdom of such a change. It would, for example, save the cost of buying houses at Gallowgatehead and it would also offer 'another direct level and elegant access to the Town, particularly the middle and west parts of it by George's Street'. They drew attention to 'the present narrow and steep access by the Gallowgate'. The Inverurie trustees, after setting up a committee to consider the proposed route, unanimously endorsed the George Street route. In April 1799 the county trustees also gave their backing to it.

But the controversy rumbled on, and in August 1801 a long open letter to the county trustees was published in the *Aberdeen Journal,* urging that Charles Abercrombie's line of road from Kittybrewster to the Gallowgate should be pressed ahead. In January 1802 the Inverurie committee were authorised to go ahead and make the road. From then on, travellers from Inverurie could make up their minds either to enter Aberdeen by the old Gallowgate route or by George Street. Today, ironically, George Street is blocked off from Union Street, the city's main artery, and a torrent of traffic pours down a dual carriageway on Cassie-end.

There were crofts on Castlehill at one time. George Fraser, in his *Historical Aberdeen,* written in 1905, said that the land in the neighbourhood of the Castle-hill, like the other land within the town's Inner Marches, was apportioned into 'crofts', or sections, each of which came to have a distinctive name. He gave the word 'crofts' in quotes, which seemed to put a question mark over the type of holdings on the hill. They were, in fact, narrow strips of land, which Diana Morgan described in her book *Round About Mounthooly* as being 'little more than plotties'.

Fraser said that each of the crofts had a distinct name. In 1411, the adjacent crofts on the north side of Castlehill were Gala Croft, Friar's Croft and Fill-the-Cap. He added that the names of other crofts in those early days could only be guessed at, but the lands on the south side underwent comparatively little change prior to the sixteenth century.

The name Fill-the-Cap on Castlehill made me take a deep breath. This was a name that had plagued me through all my research into the place names of Aberdeen and the north-east. Fill-the-Cap, Fill-the-Cop, Fill-the-Caup – it came in all variations. I found it on gravestones, on a ruined croft, on the site of a kirk in Banff, in a city street, but no one, not even the experts, came up with the answer to what it meant and where it had originated.

I kept on trying. I found two Fill-the-Cops in a 1591 charter regarding property belonging to Deer Monastery, which the king had granted to George, Earl Marischal, Lord Keith, and William Keith, his eldest son. It included 'the Croft called Fill-the-Cop (occupied by Agnes Menzies and Gilbertum Falconer, his sub-tenant) in the east territory of Aberdeen (between the Croft of John Irving of Kyncowsie (Kincausie), also called Fill-the Cop, and the Futhies Myre.'

This ancient charter threw up names that were almost as mystifying as Fill-the-Cap. For instance, near the Deneburne (Denburn), not far from the Grammar School gymnasium, there was a croft called the Sowcroft, while another croft had the mind-boggling name of Cwnyng-hareillis. It was occupied by a Patrick Gray and John Dortie, his tenant, 'in the east territory of Aberdeen between the Lynks and Crofts of David Menzies called Gallowhills'.

Of course, most place names taxed your brain. Fraser mentioned two which were troublesome to onomastic addicts – Hardweird Croft and its neighbour Sillieweird Croft in the Upper Denburn area. 'Sillie' had been taken to mean 'sillak' or 'sic-like,' meaning 'similar', but similar to what, asked Fraser. Similar to the Hardweird?

It was no use guessing. Speculation in place-names, said Fraser, was inadmissible. I wondered if he had speculated on Fill-the-Cap. When he was writing about Constitution Street he said it was 'made partly on a piece of ground known from ancient days by the name of Fill-the-Cap'. A public intimation in the local newspaper said that the new street was 'now made out through the ground of Fill-the-Cap'. But Aberdeen's librarian, who knew every neuk and cranny in the city, and had probed and poked at the origin of thousands of them, was stumped by Fill-the-Cap. He wrote in a footnote: 'The meaning of the name "Fill-the-Cap" has been discussed, but so far without any satisfactory result.' That was ninety-three years ago.

26

HAUD YER FEET

When ye come t' Ellendoon
Moitus is the nearest toon,
When ye come t' Clashnadarroch
Haud yer feet, the road's narrow.

When I first read this old place rhyme I wanted to test it – to find out if this mysterious road was still as narrow as it was on the day the verse was written. First, however, I had to discover where Ellendoon was, and the curious Moitus, and to do that I had to make my way north to Clashindarroch, somewhere near the Tap o' Noth.

This is an area rich in place-name lore. Half-way up the Tap o' Noth is the strangely-named Clochmaloo, a spur of perpendicular rock jutting out from the side of the hill, about 30 feet high, while behind, standing clear of the hill, it is 7 or 8 feet high. The place-name expert James Macdonald thought it a 'puzzling name,' but decided it was 'the stone of Moluach'. In other words, it was dedicated to Saint Moluach, whose name took different forms, including Molew.

From the Tap o' Noth the Clashindarroch Forest sweeps over the hills to the north and west. Maps of this vast forestland make fascinating reading, for there are names here to tease the imagination. Cat Craigs, for instance, or Blind Stripe, or the Wormy Hillock. Cat Craigs are jagged rocks on the south-west slope of the Hill of Kirkney and Blind Stripe is a burn that disappears underground.

Clochmaloo, the Stone of St Moulag, famous Celtic missionary, which rises near the summit of the Tap o' Noth.

Wormy Hillock is a circular hillock near the foot of the Ealaiche Burn. It was said at one time to be the 'grave-mound of a dragon' which was slain at this spot by some unknown St George. There was a surrounding dyke, 150 feet in circumference and 5 feet high. This was said to be a pend for protecting sheep in stormy weather, which put an end to romantic stories about dragons.

There are two Watchman hills – Meikle Watchman and Little Watchman. The original name of one of these hills was *Torran-buachaille*, 'knoll of the herd', which was said to be 'a fanciful name often given to spur of a hill or projecting rock'. There is also a Kye Hill, a name that comes from the old Gaelic *caedh*, 'a quagmire'; another theory is that the hill was covered with heather and unsuitable for feeding kye (cows). Some hills and cairns are named after people, among them Mrs Hay's Cairn and Kemp's Hill, but nothing is known about Mr Kemp or Mrs Hay. There is also a Carlin Hill; a carlin was an old woman, a witch, or a hag.

James Macdonald in his *Place-Names in Strathbogie*, wrote about a 'lost' village in the heart of Clashindarroch Forest. It was situated at a pasture farm called Bogincloch. In the old days there was a familiar custom of turning out horses during the summer into a glen or a hill where there was a privilege of common pasturage.

At Bogancloch – *Bog-an-cloiche*, 'the stony bog' – huge boulders were scattered over an area of about four acres of elevated ground surrounded by bogs or land which was formerly boggy. The stones ranged from 2ft to 6ft long, 2ft to 4ft wide, and 2ft to 3ft in thickness.

Bogincloch Lodge is shown on the OS map. At the end of a ridge near the lodge, within an area of less than two acres, were the foundations of between thirty and forty houses, 'or erections of some sort.' These foundations were formed of rough boulders without any dressing and were either square or oblong, some rounded at the corners. They varied in size from 8ft to 14ft long and from 5ft to 10ft wide. Under a deposit of loamy soil the areas appeared to be all neatly paved. A number of the erections were double, with doorways at either end.

Macdonald thought that the most southerly erection was a byre, judging from its length and the fact that two of the three compartments opened into a semi-circular enclosure. Here and there were similar enclosures, probably for holding cattle.

'A burn at some little distance has been diverted from its course and led by a cutting of considerable depth through the centre of the place,' wrote Macdonald. 'The popular idea is that the place is the site of an ancient village, and it is pointed out that it is situated at an angle of the glen so as to command a view both of the Tap and the Buck.'

The diverted burn must have been the Kirkney Water, which passes close to the lodge. Not shown on the map is a place called Claymellat, which is said to be 'obsolete.' Macdonald thought that the name meant 'a clay mallet-shaped hill'. There are no roads into Clashindarroch's 'lost' village but the area is criss-crossed with forest paths.

From Boganloch a track runs east to two spots marked on the map as Old Forest and New Forest. This was an area between the Hill of Cloiche Dubh and the Hill of Oldmerdrum known simply as The Forrests. It indicated, said Macdonald, along with other names, the wooded nature of the country in old times and its importance. In 1600, it was laid down that 'the woid of Kirnie was aluayes to my lordis awn use'. Mention was also made of the Huntly Rental of 1600, which referred to the 'two forests of Mytice'. Moitus, Mytice – here was a reminder of the old place rhyme that first brought me to Clashindarroch Forest.

'When ye come t' Ellendoon . . .' The Ellendoon in the place rhyme is given in the OS map as Ellan-duan, which Alexander said was not the sound. The name applied to a sloping piece of hill pasture in the Kirkney valley. The probable origin is *alltan donn*, 'brown little burn', and the burn is shown on the map coming down from its source on the north side of the Tap o' Noth.

This is the way the place-rhyme writer must have come, down the north slope of the Tap to the brown burn. He would have had to cross the Kirkney Water to get to Mytice, the 'nearest toun' (ferm toun), which sits at the end of a rough farm track to Clashindarroch, where a well is marked on the map.

From here the road is tarred, running north for about three miles until it joins the Gartly-Huntly road. It follows the twists and turns of the Kirkney Water, past Gordon's Haugh and the Factor's Skur, through the Glen of Tillyminnate and on by Darnie Heugh and Calnacreich . . . names, names, names, they dazzle and dumbfound you. Darnie Heugh is from the Scots *darn* or *dern,* 'secret', 'concealed', and Tillyminnate is from *Tulach mennat,* knoll of the swelling.

The road is clearly an improvement on the one our place-name poet wrote about, but it would still be best to heed his words – 'Haud yer feet, the road's narrow.'

27

LYNE O' SKENE

Auld-farran' canty bodies.　　　　　　　　　*well-behaved; cantry*
Better never ha'e I seen;
Auld-farran' canty bodies
Dwalls into the Lyne o' Skene.

The Lyne o' Skene lies about eight miles west of Aberdeen. It looks south to the mile-long Loch of Skene – 'a lake of considerable extent, the lake of Skene,' said the Statistical Account of Scotland for 1791–1799. The Lyne, which is one of four small villages in the parish, is cradled by a rash of farms and crofts with names like Terryvales, Breamy, Lauchintilly and Corskie. These were the homes of the 'auld-farrand' folk mentioned in the verse above, written by a wandering packman called William Chisholm.

This humble packman made a remarkable impression on the people of the Lyne. He had little education and was put to work as a heckler (flax-dresser), but the job affected his health and he decided to make a living as a packman, travelling the country with 'a little pack of stationery kind of goods'.

He was an intelligent man and a great lover of poetry. He knew Burns almost by heart, as well as the works of Byron, Shakespeare, Scott and others, and he could quote almost any chapter and passage in the Bible. He was a friend of William Thom, the Inverurie weaver poet.

He travelled all over the country, and across to Ireland, living the life of a tramp, and he often gave graphic descriptions of his adventures 'on the road'. He had to mix with other gangrels and hobos, many of whom were making a lot of money, and he himself learned how to do well out of his pack. He was said to be kind and cheerful, and a sweet singer. His listeners often melted into tears when he sung.

Chisholm's travels took him to the Lyne of Skene in 1854 and he decided to settle there. Life was 'cosh an' cosy' in this quiet backwater. He got to know the folk in the farms and crofts around the Lyne. They were 'open-handed and kindly-hearted' and, he said, they would 'fill my purse an' teem my pack'. They, in turn, took a liking to this packman who could quote Burns and the Bible and bring tears to their eyes with his songs.

He spent his declining years in this scattered community and died there in February 1862. Shortly before his death he wrote a poem about 'The Bodies o' the Lyne of Skene.' There were nine verses and a chorus:

Ye powers o'rhyme! Gi'e me a lift
To string thegither twa' three line,
About some frien's that I ha'e here,
That's lang been guid to me an' mine;
Gi'e me the power to raise a lilt,
To show my thoughts an' feelings keen –
Wi' gratefu' glee I fain wad sing
The bodies o' the Lyne o' Skene.

Frae Castle Fraser tae Braid Straik
I've drawn mony a shinin' groat,
Kintore an' Echt hae often helped
To brighten up my gloomy lot.
The twa Afflochs, the Terryvales,
The bonnie Newton, an' Greystane
May weel come ben – they're brithers to
The bodies o' the Lyne o' Skene.

There's Lauchintilly an' Scrapehard
The blessings o' the puir ha'e won,
An' better folk ye winna get
Than Drumnaheath an' Tillybin;
The Letter gars my spirits glow;
In Wardis I fin' aye a friend;
An' Breamy, kind, may weel compare
Wi' bodies o' the Lyne o' Skene.

The gardener lads I canna pass,
For deeds o' kindness never slack –
Baith auld an' young ha'e often helped
To fill my purse an' teem my pack.
The auldest frien' that I ha'e here,
Wi' heart like steel, sae true an' keen,
Lang may he live to crack an'joke
Wi' bodies o' the Lyne o' Skene.

For Craigiedarg, I'll ne'er forget,
Wi' kindly welcome sets you doun;
An' Bervie, Corskie, Wateron,
Shall mingle in my hamely tune,
Back Ward, Blue Park, the merchant's folk
Hae ever kind an' canty been;
An' lang may Marshal's humour please
The bodies o' the Lyne o' Skene.

There's tailors, souters, wrights, an' smiths,
Like brithers, kind ha'e been to me;
An' lealer hearts ye wadna fin'
Atween the banks o' Don an' Dee.
The Fornets gran' I maun bring in
Afore my ravel't rhyme be deen,
An' cottage bodies warm my heart
Like bodies o' the Lyne o' Skene.

When frosty fogs bedim the moss,
An' little robin's nearly dumb;
Or storms drive o'er frae Wardis braes,
An' roar like thunder o'er the lum;
Though tempests sweep the leafless woods,
An' bend an' brak the firs sae green,
Yet cosh an' cosy here I sit
'Mang bodies o' the Lyne o' Skene.

May corn an' cattle ever thrive,
An' kirns an' girnals ne'er gae deen.
An' layin' hens an' heavy calves,
An' kebbucks like the harvest meen,
An' tattie pits like giants' graves,

An' kail an' clover ever green,
An' buckin' stacks an' towerin' rucks
Be ever in the Lyne o' Skene.

I went off to find out more about this land where a kebbuck (a cheese) looked like a harvest moon and where tattie pits were as big as giants' graves. I also wanted to find out if the folk of the Lyne were the same 'aul' farrant, canty' folk that their forefathers were a century and a half ago.

The Lyne of Skene is pronounced the Line of Skene by locals. The word comes from the Gaelic *loinn,* a meadow, field or enclosure. James Macdonald, in his *Place Names of West Aberdeenshire,* said that it meant a 'line' or straight row of houses, which was probably a good description of the village.

The *Imperial Gazetteer of Scotland,* published about the time William Chisholm was writing his 'Bodies o' the Lyne o' Skene', gave a long piece about Skene, 'a parish containing a post-office station of its own name,' but made no mention at all of the Lyne. The Lyne's neighbour, the Kirkton, is a rural metropolis compared to the Lyne, but the Lyne is no quiet backwater, for huge lorries thunder through it on their way from Kintore to Dunecht. William Chisholm wrote:

Kintore an' Echt hae often helped
to brighten up my gloomy lot.

But the road between the two places does nothing to brighten up the lot of anyone trying to cross the road. Christina Machray, who has been at the Lyne for forty years, told me that at peak times it was almost impossible to get from one side to the other.

It was at the cross-roads, where the former school has been converted into a community centre, that I met Christina, who was waiting for the Portsoy fish van to arrive on its weekly visit. She had heard about the Chisholm poem and put me in touch with Roy Lilly, who lived up the road and was an expert on cars and cornkisters – and hopefully, the bodies o' Lyne o' Skene. While huge lorry-hopping vehicles went roaring past us, I stood with Roy quoting passages from the 'Bodies' and asking about people and places in the poem, or 'my hamely tune', as Chisholm called it. Greystane was 'a puckle crofts', Breamy, which had totally baffled me, turned out to be Broomhill; Wardis was the local pronounciation of Wardhouse, and Waterton, to my surprise, was Dunecht. According to Alexander, Dunecht meant the *dun* of the Echt, the ancient hill fort on the

Barmekin. In comparatively recent times it had become the name of the estate and 'also of the roadside village more properly called the Waterton of Echt'.

Some of the farms, Lauchintilly, for instance, 'the loch of the knoll', and Tillybin, 'the knoll of judgement, i.e. of a court', were occupied by Andersons. The Anderson family seemed to loom large in the Skene area. but I found out more about them later. The local wit in Chisholm's day seems to have been a man called Marshal – 'And lang may Marshal's humour please the bodies o' the Lyne o' Skene' – but, unlike the packman's verse, Mr Marshal and his humour were long forgotten.

There were lines in the poem which seemed to go back to a time when the Lyne was bigger and busier:

> There's tailors, souters, wrights, and smiths,
> Like brithers, kind ha'e been to me.

There are no tailors, souters, wrights and smiths in the village now, but a building across the road from Roy Lyall's house had been the old smiddy. Roy's grandfather, Davie Lyall, had been the souter at the Lyne. He died during the First World War.

Chisholm's poem said that 'better folk ye winna get than Drumnaheath an' Tillybin'. For almost three hundred years Drumnaheath has been in the hands of the Carney family, but the steading there has been turned into houses and Donald Carney lives in a modern building, Whinndale, not far from his ancestral home. It is an intriguing thought that there was a Carney in Drumnaheath when our packman-poet was selling his wares there. Like his forefathers, Don Carney ploughs the fields, yokes his Clydesdales, hyows his neeps, and herds his cattle, but now he does it on film. Fifteen years ago he set up a company, Carney & Lyall (Roy Lyall) Productions Ltd, which produces farming videos that go all over the world.

It began as a hobby, he says, and now it has over five hundred hours of unique material, much of which has never been recorded on film before. He is bringing alive the sights and sounds of the ferm touns of a century ago. The people featured in the videos are not actors, but the ordinary folk of Aberdeenshire, using spontaneously the language of their forefathers, the Doric dialect of the North-east. His first video was 'Meal and Ale at East Letter Fairm'. East Letter farm is only a short distance from the Lyne. The name comes from *leiter,* a hillside. The meal and ale was held in the barn and Don told me of the folk who 'cam' in aboot' that night,

The cover for the video of 'The Meal and Ale at East Letter Fairm'.

dressed in period clothes, with some women making dumplings and others making cheese. The video was an outstanding success and it is still selling today.

Two other farms that caught my eye were Lauchintilly and Scrapehard. These were farms that had won 'the blessings o' the puir'. There was little doubt that in Chisholm's time life at Scrapehard would have been difficult and demanding, yet whoever worked it in those far-off days had gone out of their way to help 'the puir'. I had seen a number of Scrapehards in my travels, but I had never heard of the Scrapehard in Skene.

Roy Lyall pointed out Lauchintilly and Scrapehard away in the distance, telling me to go down the road to Kintore and turn off at Leylodge. From there I went up past Drumnaheath and Tillybin, heading into the back-o'-beyond as far as I could see, with the road showing marked signs of deterioration the farther up I went. Beyond Lauchintilly I passed a sign saying 'Private Road' and after that the road got steeper and rougher, and then a big four-wheel drive came rumbling down the hill and stopped beside me. The driver asked if he could help, mentioning that he had just come down from the Glack, the farm at the top of the hill.

'Are you an Anderson?' I asked. He was one of the Andersons I had heard about – Bill Anderson, who farmed at Lauchintilly. He listened as I told him I was looking for Scrapehard, and why. 'I'll tell you what to do,' he said. 'That's Scrapehard down there,' pointing to the roof of a farm building that could just be seen at the bottom of the road, 'go down there and see my Uncle Jimmy. He's ninety-three, but he'll tell you all you want to know about Scrapehard. Auntie Betty will be there as well. She's ninety-one.'

So off he went with a wave of his hand and down I went to Scrapehard. Bill Anderson had sounded a note of caution. If Uncle Jimmy was in the mood he would talk to me freely, but, on the other hand, he might not. Auntie Betty came to the door and took me in to meet Uncle Jimmy, who seemed to me to be one of the 'auld-farrant, canty bodies' glorified in William Chisholm's song.

They were a lovely couple. Jimmy said he was 'nae sae good at walkin', and he was also a bit deaf, but I never heard him complaining. Betty bore her ninety years well. She had a sharp mind and a fine sense of humour. When I first met her she wore an old-fashioned 'peenie' with two big pockets on the front of it. 'I'll tell you fit it's fine for,' she said. 'If ye let fa' a spoon it lands in een o' the pockets!'

They told me how the Andersons of Midmar had come to Glack in

Jimmy and Betty Anderson at their croft
at Scrapehard in the Lyne of Skene.

1908. Jimmy was born there and he and his brother Bill worked for their father. 'They widna be on the farm the day if Jimmy hidna ca'd himself' deen working it,' said Betty. 'It was doon tae naething jist after the First World War.' Later, he took over the farm from his father. 'He got the Glack,' said Betty.

The Andersons also got Lauchintilly and before they were married they took over Scrapehard. 'I niver thocht I wid bide at Scrapehard,' said Jimmy. But they did and it was 'an afa mess' when they got it. Now they have been there for forty-six years. Originally, Scrapehard was 'up at the heid o' the hill', in other words, the Glack, but the name came to apply to the old croft down the hill.

The name Scrapehard conjures up pictures of crofts tottering on the brink of poverty, scraping a meage living out of hard, unyielding land, but there are other interpretations. *Chambers Scots Dictionary* said it was 'one who has difficulty in making ends meet'. William Alexander wrote, 'The dialect says Scrap Hard,' and Betty Anderson told me that she had a cousin who had worked in the Mitchell Library in Glasgow and he believed that the name was Scrapyaird, which meant high ground.

Whatever the explanation, few people are likely to rush into buying a croft called Scrapehard. Jimmy told me, with just a hint of delight in his voice, what happened when the estate tried to rent out the house. 'They couldna get it let,' he said, 'so the factor ca'd it Nether Lauchintilly!'

'How did they get it changed back?' I asked.

'Its nae changed back,' said Betty. 'It's still Lauchintilly.'

That explained why I had never found Scrapehard on the OS map when I looked for it before going to the Lyne of Skene. I saw Nether Lauchintilly, but it meant nothing to me. By all accounts, it means nothing to anyone else, least of all the folk who live there, for everybody calls it 'Scrapes'. Roy Lilly spoke about Scrapes when he was talking to me and Jimmy and Betty always call it Scrapes. Place names mirror the history of a community, so perhaps some wise head will one day change it back to what it should be – Scrapehard.

I left the house with Jimmy and Betty and sat on a dyke to enjoy the view. Round the front of the house I was shown a maple tree standing up straight and proud. Betty said that Jimmy had 'brocht it back fae Canada in his pocket'. From where we were we could see the Line, as they call it, and a vast panorama of farmland, with sheep and cattle grazing on it.

Up above us the 'private road' went on its way, potholed and perilous, with thistles rising shoulder high on one side of it and gorse and broom choking it on the other side. The road swings past Scrapes and ziz-zags steeply up to the Glack. I drove up it to see William Anderson, Bill Anderson's son, who works the farm with his father. It is an old farm, with big, weary looking farm buildings, dark and unwelcoming, although the farmhouse itself seemed friendly enough. Bill came out with his collie pup, Jet, and his wife Donna followed with their two children, Lewis, who was five, and Claire, who was two. I wanted a picture of them, so Claire was hauled off to the sink because her Mum thought she was 'muckit'.

I could understand why they said Glack was on the 'heid o' the hill'. From the farm the Andersons have an unrivalled bird's-eye view of the countryside, and behind them a green field pushes its way up to Glack Wood on top of the hill. I was reluctant to leave the Glack. The word is both Scots and Gaelic: *glac*, a hollow or cut between hills. I thought of the turbulent road down below. I asked William if they were going to repair it? He thought this over and said, 'We're thinking about it.' He thought it best to continue along the road, which would take me to Dunecht.

Before I left Scrapehard I mentioned to old Jimmy Anderson that I was heading for a place called Woggle Farm. He knew where it was, in Kinellar,

William and Donna Anderson with their children Lewis and Claire at
Glack Farm.

north-east of the Lyne of Skene and not far from the Tyrebagger. So I said
goodbye to Jimmy and Betty, hoping I would see them again some day.
When I left, I remembered what William Chisholm said about the people at
Scrapeyard – 'Better folk ye winna get'. That was a century and a half ago,
but he might well have been speaking about the folk who live there today.

The Land of Waggles isn't easy to find. Waggle folk lives in different
parts of the North-east. You'll find them in Birse, which is said to have 'a
certain feeling of remoteness and wildness', or up on Deeside, and you'll
find them in suburban Aberdeen. You'll also find them in Buchan, the land
of 'peat-bogs and puddock steels'. In fact, you are liable to come upon
Waggles and Woggles if you are anywhere near a bog.

'Woggle' is the old Scots word for a bog and 'waggle' is a quaking bog.
Other variations are Wuggle, Wagley and Wagglehead. William Alexander
noted a Wagley in Newhills, a parish that has been largely swallowed up by
the city. He thought the original name was Waggle-ley, the 'ley' meaning
open grassland. The Woggle Farm in Kinellar is owned by Charles
Marshal, of Caskieben, of Marshall Trailers, and there is a Woggle Cottage
and a Woggle Burn. When I asked a passer-by how to get to the farm he
said it was down the Woggle road.

There seemed to be Woggles all over the place, but I found nothing to suggest that this was or had been an exceptionally boggy area. On the other hand, there is a Hillhead of Boghead on the Muir of Kinellar. There is also an Ellismoss not far from Woggle Farm. Confusingly, Alexander said it was called 'Alehouse, in place names', so if you go there you can drop into an alehouse for a drink instead of sinking up to your knees in a bog.

I thought the Woggles were being ousted by the Womblies, for less than a mile from the Hill of Boghead are two farms called Womblehill and South Womblehill. The name, which goes back as far as 1525, is pronounced 'Wummle-hill'.

Buchan is surely the Land of Waggles, for in Cuminestown there is a Waggle Hill, which has a Waggle Cairn on it. I thought this must have some special significance. I saw it on the Internet, put there by a mapping company called Multi-map. The north end of the hill is called Tryst Hill because the Cuminestown Tryst used to be held there, but I approached it from the south, partly because there was a farm in the area called Sprottyneuk. I have always thought that this North-east corner had more quaint, lugubrious and funny place names than anywhere else in the country.

Sprottyneuk was a place where sprots grew, a sprot being 'a jointed-leaved rush', which suggested boggy land. Not far from that was another farm called Rush-head. I discovered later that there were three farms at the *north* end of Waggle Hill called Boghead, Rashypans and Moss-side, so from whatever direction I approached the hill it looked as if I had found the Land of Waggles.

The roads around Cuminestown bend and twist like an agitated rattlesnake, but when they finally turned north and straightened out I found myself in the Howe of Teuchar, another curious place name. 'Teuch' means tough and the *Concise Scots Dictionary* gives 'teuchter' as 'an uncouth, countrified person'. There was a small community in the Howe and some of the buildings looked as if they had seen better days, but the first house I came to had two large pillars at the entrance that might have come from the laird's howff. On top of them were two prancing sculpted horses.

When I stopped the car I saw a lone figure marching along the road towards me. 'Can you tell me where Waggle Hill is?' I asked. He pointed to the fields that slanted uphill from the roadside and said, 'That's it!'. Then he pointed to a house that could be seen on the top of the hill and said, 'That's Waggle Hill Croft.'

His name was Davie Rochester. He was a Geordie who, retired, had come to Waggle country ten years ago. He said he was a bit of a DIY man and had done up a cottage on the narrow road that led up to Waggle Hill Croft. He called it Thistledown. He had walked all over the hill but had never seen the cairn. He thought it might be in the woods that stretched along the flat summit of the hill. The author Nigel Tranter, who mentioned the 'very slight eminence' of the Waggle Hill, only 585 feet, in one of his books, said the Waggle Cairn was on the northern flank of the hill.

Davie Rochester seemed happy with his lot in Waggle country. He said they were trying to open a community centre for the local folk, probably in the school, now closed. I watched him march off down the road and then I drove up past Thistledown to the croft. There was no one at home, but the owner arrived when I was there. His name was Ian Freeguard and he turned out to be another Englishman, this time from Herefordshire. Like Davie, he had never seen the cairn and also thought it might be hidden away in the wood. He said it was very boggy in the wood.

When Davie pointed out the croft to me he spoke about the building with the green corrugated roof. It had low windows and doors and Ian said it was a steading. It stood beside the old farmhouse, which had been there for a hundred years. I couldn't help thinking that it was an unusual

The outbuilding at Waggle Hill Croft – a steading or a 'chaumer'.

type of steading and that at some time in the distant past it had housed people. My own view was that it has been a chaumer, a sleeping place for farm workers.

Ian spoke ecstatically about the view from his hilltop home. From it you can see the familiar peaks of Bennachie, twenty miles away, and the hills at Dufftown forty miles away, and you can turn full circle and see a vast panorama of farmland, its fields turned brown by an unexpectedly hot summer. I thought of the farm folk I had met at the Lyne of Skene and remembered what Christina Machray had said – 'There's more English folk here than there are Scots.' Well, I had a suspicion that it was also happening in the Land of Waggles.

Ian Freeguard at Waggle Hill Croft.

28

GHOST ROADS

The old hill trails have become ghost roads, but their names linger on: the Ca', the Winny Turn, the Byoorn Road, the Balloch, the Cadgers' Road, the Strone Yarrich – unfathomable names that point the way to the past. They take you to forgotten tracks and ancient hill passes and tell you about places and people of long ago.

On Deeside, for instance, the Strone Yarrich road was, and still is, part of the old military road between Crathie and the Gairn. There was a poem written by a Ballater man, Calum Mackie, which went:

Up the Darach,
An ower Stranyarrich,
Up ower the Shenval,
Lift up yer kilt,
Tomintoul an time til't.

The Darach Road was the road going west out of Ballater below Craigendarroch and the Shenval, *An Sean-bhaile,* was an old farm-town north-east of Gairnshiel. For years the farmhouse has been disintegrating, its skeleton clinging ghoulishly to the edge of the road, as if it knew it was the last survivor of the township that was there.

John Fleming, the last of the Flemings in the glen, worked the Shenval croft, ploughing the hard, stony ground with a horse and a stot. A few years ago, Rab Bain, one of Deeside's great characters, leased the grazing on Shenval and two other old crofts, Richarkarie and Torran.

So life goes on, and the cars and coaches puff up the Shenval brae on their way to Tomintoul, while their occupants gawk in disbelief at the roadside ruins and you think you can hear a voice from the past saying, 'Lift up yer kilt, Tomintoul an time til't.'

William Alexander thought that the name Strone Yarrich may originally have referred to the 'fairly conspicuous Strone (hill) at the Gairn end above Braenaloin'. The Strone Yarrich road from Gairn to Crathie forks below Piperhole. One end joins the Deeside road at a house once known as Chrystal's, the other at Tyanabaich.

If you come south by the Shenval and down the Gairn to the North Deeside road, turning east to Willie Meston's inn at Coilacreich, you will pass the Winny Turn (Windy Turn), a blowy corner on the main road between the Brig o Gairn and Coilacreich. You'd best take care there because William Alexander said in his place-name book that the name Winny Turn was 'very appropriate'. Michie, in his *Deeside Tales,* named this corner Luimnaghui (*Leum na Gaoithe*), which literally means 'leap of the wind'.

For many years I had a caravan at Tarland, not far from the Pressendye hill ridge, the barrier between the Howe of Cromar and Leochel-Cushnie. The drovers came along that high-rise route on their way to markets in the south, but there was also a busy traffic of local people going over the hill to Cushnie and Towie. They used the route by Badnachraskie, one of the old thoroughfares between Cromar and Strathdon. It followed a line going west of the present main Logie-Coldstone road, then picked up the Tarland-Migvie road and pushed on to Deskrie and the Mill of Ennot. In 1724 it was described as 'a steep hill called Baadchraskie' and 'Badcraskie' is still said to be the most authentic pronunciation.

There are a lot of 'bad' roads in the place-name world – Bad Leanna, a stance for drovers crossing a hill at Corgarff; Bad na Cuaiche in Glen Ernan; Badhabber, a moss at the head of the Girnock, and so on. There is a Muckle Steen of Badhabber, a large boulder by the side of the Crathie-Loch Muick road. The word 'bad' actually means a clump; Bad Leanna, for instance, is *bnad leathann,* 'broad clump', and there is the curious Bad na Cuaiche, 'the clump of the cuckoo'. Badenyon in Glenbucket is from *Baan eoin,* 'bird's clump'.

One that was well-known was Badnagoach, a farm on Deskry-side, which was a well-known resting place for drovers. The farmer there was called Bednie. A. R. Haldane, in *The Drove Roads of Scotland,* said that in 1948 there were still people living on Donside who remembered cattle climbing to the watershed and resting at Badnagoach near the top of the Deskry Water.

Back in the nineteenth century the Valuation Rolls showed the name as Badnagaugh or Badengauch. The original Gaelic was *Badan gaothach,* the 'windy clump or hamlet', which suggested that there was a settlement there. James Macdonald said, 'Like most of the *gauchs,* this place is situated at the junction of two burns, and exposed to every gale of wind from whatever quarter it may come.'

From Logie-Coldstone another track called the Cach went up the hill behind the farm of Groddie. The name came from *cadha,* 'a hill pass'. Groddie itself is from *grodaidh,* a rotten place, a stagnant marsh or bog. I remember squelching my way up to Byron's 'Morven of the Snows' many years ago, not knowing about Groddie's reputation as a quagmire. The farm and its crops were being eaten away by rabbits. But things have improved since that time (see Chapter 12).

The Bealach Dearg is probably the best-known of the old hill passes on Deeside. The Red Pass, as it is called, ran from Invercauld over to the Gairn and was part of the old foot and drove road from Tomintoul to the south. The southern end of the pass went out of use a long time ago. It originally left the Fearder valley, passed an extinct croft called Corrour, and went on to the mouth of the Sluggan burn, where it crossed the Dee beside Braemar Castle.

The old pass to Builg went north on the west side of Culardoch, but a number of other tracks pass it on the east side and go down to the Gairn. It is an interesting area. Up the Fearder burn is Auchtavan, where the Queen Mother had a shiel. It is still there.

Away from the hills, there are plenty of old roads with tongue-twisting names, but I cast my vote for a name that is down-to-earth and made up by the folk who lived there – the Sooth an' North, they called it. It was the main road from the Bridge of Alford to the Mill of Dess. The road was finished in 1817 and superseded the older thoroughfare between Bridge of Alford and Kincardine O'Neil, which is still traceable.

The old whisky roads hug their secrets when you stravaig in the hills. One of the most fascinating is the old Mounth road from 'Innermarkie to Canakyle on Deesyde'. Canakyle or Candecaill is now known as Dee Castle. Travellers going this way made a giant 'leap-frog' from Glentanar into Glenmark, stopping at the inn at Coirebhruach to quench their thirst before going over Mount Keen.

A rickle of stones is all that remains of the old inn. Nearby was the Shiel

The ruins of Coirebhruach Inn at the head of Glen Tanar on Deeside.

The Shiel of Tana at the head of Glen Tanar. It was mysteriously burned to the ground.

of Tanna, a shooting lodge well-known to hillwalkers, but it was burned to the ground, some say by vandals. The stable at the Shiel had twin stalls and on the wall large wooden pegs for hanging harness. I once found a message there telling me that a George Sutherland had stabled his horse at the Shiel in 1890. He came back in 1922 'enjoying a picnic'.

Here a few more unusual and interesting road names:

Bockie Howe – A bockie is a hobgoblin, a mischievous spirit. There are two Bockie Howes on Deeside, one in a hollow by a sharp bend in the road up Glen Muick, the other west of the Coilacreich Inn.

The Pey – The brae on the road west of Deecastle on Deeside is called the Red Pey. It is said to come from the Scots *path*, pronounced peth, which the Scots dictionary says is 'a steep track or road leading down a ravine and up the other side'.

The Skair – The Skair Brae is in the Kintore area. It is a steep bit on the old road between Nethermill and Muir of Kinellar.

Skatebrae – This was a brae at Auchterless with a *scawt*, a scabby or broken surface.

The Sinnerins – This is a fork on the Skene and Echt roads six miles out of Aberdeen. The name, a dialect one, means the parting, from the Scots *sinner, to* part company.

The Clash Brae – A long brae on the Aberdeen-Tarland road. The 'clash' comes from a ravine at the top of the brae. 'Slack' has the same meaning, as in the Slack of Tillylodge (see Chapter Four).

Isaacside – This was the name of a road in Auchindoir, but who Isaac was is a mystery. It was said to be the name of a burn, now called the Packet, which runs down the west side of Lunsden village.

Cadgers' Road – There was a Cadgers' Road at Culsalmond and a Cadgerford at Peterculter. Old maps show many of the old routes taken by packmen and travelling salesmen.

Fisherford – This place at Auchterless was on the line of a Cadger's Road near Pitmedden called the Fisher Walk.

The Creel Road – Creels of peats on horseback were carried over this track from peat-mosses at Roar, near Logie-Coldstone. There was also a Cristie Moss Road south-west of the Linn of Dee.

The Still Road – A road running from Tornauran, south-west of Abergeldie, to Balmoral.

The Street of Monaltrie – A former row of houses north-east of Inver.

The Fog House Path – A path near the Garrawalt Falls in Ballochbuie

Forest. There were a number of 'fog houses' – small summer houses – on Deeside estates, usually built in mossy areas.

Tangland Ford – A well-known crossing of the Ythan. There is a bridge there now. Pratt said that 'Tangland' was a corruption of St Englat, the tutular saint of Tarves.

The Braid Milestone – This is the name of a milestone at the junction of the Peterhead and Fraserburgh roads a mile north of Pitsligo.

The Causey Mounth – The ancient pass from Aberdeen to Stonehaven. It was also known as the Cowie or Cowy Mounth, taking the name from the vanished village of Cowie and its the castle at the southern end. The old pass was once described as a 'morass'. In 1658, a Captain Franks passed over the Mounth and declared, 'Causeys uncartable, pavements unpracticable.'

Causeway Mounth Farm at the start of the old Mounth road from Aberdeen to Stonehaven.

29

GOLDEN PUMPHEL

The first time I heard about the Golden Pumphel, which was said to be found in the Towie hills, I thought it might be a bird, or maybe some strange, exotic plant, and then I wondered if it was a crystal or 'stone' similar to those that had been dug up in the Cairngorms. It made me think of something I had once read in MacFarlane's *Geographical Collection:* 'Kairne Gorum, a famous hill, which is four miles high; Gold hath been found here. The Hill aboundeth with excellent Crystall.'

The old Statistical Account of Scotland, published in 1795, said that the stones found in these mountains were 'as hard as any oriental gem.' There were beautiful amethysts and emeralds, though these were rare.

But Cairngorm wasn't the only hill to hold a treasure chest of precious stones. 'Amethysts are to be found on Loch-na-Garaidth; emeralds, topazes on Binn-na-Baird, and the brown kind only on Binn-na-Muick-duidh and the other mountains in these parishes.'

Well, why not Towie parish? Maybe, I thought, gold hath been found there too. The name Pumphel, the *Golden* Pumphel, had a certain ring about it. My search for the Pumphel took me to the Tillyfunter Hillock, one of a number of hillocks dotted about the hill country north of the Pressendye ridge. This particular mound was in a valley above the Mill of Culfork, east of the Lazy Well Road and the Gallows Hill.

This is sheep country and the Tillyfunter Hillock was where livestock was penned. William Alexander, in his *Place-Names of Aberdeenshire,* said, 'It overlooks the curious enclosure called the Golden Pumphel, and so may be interpreted as *tulach-phundair,* "the poinder's hillock".' The enclosure was made of earth, stone or wood. In the days before land was enclosed it held stray livestock impounded by an official, called a poinder or pundler.

There is, or was, a Pumphillford at Aberdour. The *Pumfle,* which was the same word as pinfold, was found fairly often in the name of a field.

Why, then, was this humble sheeps' pen given such an exotic name – and what was there about it that justified its description as golden? The answer is that 'pumphel' is a Scots word; not only that, according to the *Concise Scottish Dictionary,* it is a *North-east* Scots word. As for the 'golden', the Gaelic for Tillyfunter is *Tulach-fionn-doire,* 'the knoll of the light-coloured thicket'. In other words, it was the grass that put the gold into the Golden Pumphel. So much for the dream of precious stones!

Not far from the Tillyfunter Hillock is a hollow shown on maps as Claivers Howe. This was where shepherds and others 'met to enjoy a quiet gossip'. The word 'claiver' was said to be allied to the Danish *klaffe,* to slander, and the German *klaffen,* to chatter, which suggests that the conversation wasn't always full of goodwill.

'In Aberdeenshire,' wrote James Macdonald, 'claivers means idle stories, often untrue and scandalous, retailed over the country with a mischievous intention.'

Whatever scandalous chit-chat filled the air at Claivers Howe, the folk of Towie had a friendlier attitude to travellers. There was a place-rhyme couplet that went:

Gin ye gang wi' me to Towie,
Ye'll get butter in a bowie.

Towie butter must have something special in it before it was held out as a treat to passing strangers. Maybe the cows in the Golden Pumphel produced milk that gave it a special flavour. There was, after all, a farm in Rhynie called Butterybrae that got its name because there was a large yield of butter when the cows were fed on the natural pasture of the brae. The farm, which is now extinct, was one of four in the parish which in 1600 paid butter as part of the rent.

The mouth-watering quality of butter from the Towie area was vouched for by no less a person than one of the lairds of Corse. During troublesome times he went into hiding in a spot on the Corse hill called the Laird's Cham'er. He was supplied with butter from Tillyorn and he was so pleased with it that when his troubles came to an end he raised the rent of the farm by three merks.

He was also determined that his butter wouldn't get into the wrong hands. In 1644, he removed 'his haill victuals' to Fintray to keep them away from the plundering MacGregors.

There is a later version of the 'butter in a bowie' poem which offers an even greater inducement to visitors – a fish! It goes:

'Will ye go to Towie?'
Quo Fill-a-Laidle, quo Fill-a-Laidle.
'Ye'll get skate upon a plate
An' butter in a bowie.'

The North-east had a number of 'buttery' place names at one time, but most have vanished. There was a Butterwards at Glass, but it seemed to have less success with its butter. James Macdonald said it was commonly called Bitterward, which was the correct name, 'indicating the sour character of the land'.

There were two Buttery Wells, one in Banchory Devenick, the other at Belhelvie. The Belhelvie Wells was also called the Coldwater Bridge. This was the place where the old Ellon road crossed the Blackdog Burn. The traditional explanation of the name was that women carrying butter into Aberdeen market used to put their butter into the water here to cool it.

30

LIFE PRESERVERS

When Charles Murray returned to Scotland from South Africa to retire in 1924, he and his close friends formed a club called the Sit Siccars. Murray suggested the title because he thought it was 'an appropriate title for a fraternity who were probably at their best sitting'.

The club met at odd times, when the fancy took them, and it had in its ranks such notable people as Lord Boyd Orr and John Buchan, Lord Tweedsmuir. Lord Boyd Orr was secretary but he never called a meeting. Murray wrote a poem called 'Advice to the Sit-Siccars,' which ended with the lines:

> In love or in liquoir
> In case 'at ye coup,   *you fall*
> Be wise an' sit siccar –
> Ye're safe on your doup.

But not everybody wanted to sit on their doups. In the 1930s a group of Aberdeen business and professional men felt it would be better for their health to go for long walks in the country instead of going to their offices on a Saturday. They decided to form a Life Preservers Society.

There were twenty members in the society, all, as it was delicately put, 'of mature years'. The founder was William Tawse, a leading Aberdeen civil engineering contractor, who enlisted the help of James A. Parker, a member of the Cairngorm Club. Charles Murray was also a member of this fraternity, as was Dr James Fowler Tocher, a prominent geneticist and Aberdeenshire county analyst.

Parker pointed out in an article in the 'Cairngorm Club Journal' that the club's name had nothing to do with 'short sticks with loaded heads'. The only sticks they carried were walking sticks. Their season was mid-February to mid-July and the average turnout was eight members.

A list of two dozen suitable walks, each averaging twelve miles in length, was drawn up by Parker, but the society actually chalked up over 200 walks. They went up Ben Avon to see the sunrise, tramped from Loch Muick to Glen Doll, traversed the skyline of the Garvock Hills in the Mearns in a gale and drenching rain, and climbed Lochnagar. Parker did his fiftieth climb of the mountain with the society. They also came down to earth and did walks on the roads, such as a trek from Rosehearty to Strichen in February, 1939.

I first learned of the Life Preservers Society when I read *Hamewith, The Complete Poems of Charles Murray*. There was a section in it dealing with Murray's last poems. It was written by Alexander Keith in 1969 and in it he mentioned the LPS – 'another Aberdeen sodality to which Tocher and Murray adhered.' Murray had obviously decided to get off his doup.

It wasn't until a few years later that I decided to become my own Life Preserver and try out one of their walks. This was from Alford to Lumphanan. It appealed to me because it started in 'Hamewith' country, about a mile east of Alford and it followed a route where there were some

Lochnagar, climbed by the Life Preservers.

intriguing place names. Parker had written about the walk in the 'Cairngorm Journal', so I could use that as a guide and compare notes.

The Life Preservers had a raw, cold day for their walk, battling against wind, rain, snow and slush. As if that wasn't bad enough, they had to climb over what Parker called 'barbed-wire abominations'. Happily, it was a glorious morning when I set out on the walk and I had the minimum of trouble with barbed wire.

From what I could make out the Life Preservers started from a croft called Lonenwell, which came from the Scots word 'loaning', which means open space between fields, or a field road. This was a road, which took me to the first landmark, a sixteenth-century tower-house, Balfluig Castle, which the historian Nigel Tranter praised as being 'splendidly restored from ruin'.

Unfortunately, it hadn't been splendidly restored when the LPS walkers were there. They found it falling apart – 'gloomy-looking Balfluig Castle', Parker called it. He said it was 'used as a hostel for hens, living and dead'. Mrs Annie Wattie, who lived in the farmhouse of Little Endovie, told me that the castle was a roofless ruin when she first came to this corner of the Howe of Alford. The Watties had kept their manure inside it.

She also thought that Parker wasn't far off the mark when he described it as a 'hens' hostel'. At that time, a Mrs Isabella McCombie, who lived in the croft adjoining Balfluig, kept her hens in the castle. The name Balfluig (pronounced 'Baflig') came from the Gaelic *Poll fliuch*, 'a wet pool'. If the Life Preservers had known this they might have been warned in advance, for they were caught in a nasty storm which turned it into a wet pool.

Even at that early stage, they must have been wondering if this sort of thing really would preserve their lives. They never quite knew where they were and at one point the party almost disintegrated. 'Everyone knew exactly where HE was,' said Parker, 'but no two opinions were the same.'

At Little Endovie the party was in the shadow of Strone Hill. Parker wrote about the 'forbidding slopes' of the Strone. It seemed a curious comment from a member of the Cairngorm Club, for it seemed to me to be a gentle hill, much of it under cultivation.

To the east of the Strone I saw the gaunt ruined walls of the mansion of Tonley. It belonged to a family called Byres, one of whom was a noted antiquary. The origin of the name Tonley is *Tigh an leigh*, 'house of the physician'. If that distinguished member of the LSP, Dr James Fowler Tocher, had been on the Lumphanan outing he would have been interested in that.

Parker mentioned 'a decayed mansion house called Little Endovie,' but he seems to have mixed it up with Tonley. He admitted that it was by sheer luck that his members came together on the south side of the Strone.

The bold adventurers talked about packing it in and walking to the nearby Muggart Haugh Inn or even tramping to Lumsden by the main road, but Parker dismissed this as a 'cowardly suggestion'. So on they went by the barbed wire route. 'The total distance covered to date,' said Parker bitterly, 'was three statute miles plus eight barbed wire fences, an average of 2.67 per route mile.'

On the west side of the Strone is Cairnballoch, *Carn Bhealaich*, 'cairn of the pass'. 'The old line of road from the Cairn o' Mount going northwards here surmounts Cairnballoch and is spoken of as going "ower the Balloch".'

The Life Preservers pushed through a field that had become sodden with melting snow and finally came to a farm called Claymill. They were invited in to 'eat their pieces'. From there they looked across to Tillyfour and the slopes of Benaquhallie, where an old drove road went up Glen Tough. Tillyfour was the home of William McCombie, known as the King of Grazers, a pioneer of the Aberdeen-Angus breed of cattle. His fame brought Queen Victoria to Tillyfour to visit him in 1866.

It was up Benaquhallie that the weary walkers made their way, up 800 feet to the snowline of a hill whose name they couldn't even pronounce. It is, in fact, pronounced Bena-hylie. They took the east side of the hill, but I took the west side, passing an old cottar house standing in ruins not far from the top. Beyond it, the hill was split by a beautifully made dyke, running from east to west, a forgotten testimony to the art of the stone-dyker.

From here it was an easy walk down to Tullochvenus on the Tarland road. When I had a caravan at Tarland I passed Tullochvenus time and time again and often wondered what romantic story lay behind the name. Did this dreary corner of the north-east harbour a Venus, a Goddess of Love, whose story had never been told? It was a long time after I had given up caravan life that I found out. I came upon it when I was glancing through William Alexander's *Place-Names of Aberdeenshire*. It was pronounced Tulloch-veenes, with the stress on 'veen'. In 1612 it was given as Tullachwyneys and in 1616 it appeared as Tullochweinis.

'The old forms,' wrote Alexander, almost gleefully it seemed, 'make 'venus' look rather like the present-day surname Wyness'.

I imagine that the noble Life Preservers were more concerned with their wet feet and sodden clothes than they were with Venus – or, for that matter, with Mr Wyness.

From Tullochvenus I followed the Cloak Burn to Lumphanan. The path is marked on some maps as an old military road. It was one of a number of little-known routes which the north-east Mountain Trust had been exploring to establish their existence as rights-of-way. I took part in that scheme and I remember pushing my way through some overgrown path near Lumphanan.

Coming down the military road, I looked over to a road which went uphill from Lumphanan past Macbeth's Cairn and Perkhill. There is a croft up there called Sunnybrae. At one time, old Willie Littlejohn, one of my mother-in-law's relatives, was tenant there. He and his wife Nan were kindly, friendly folk – even with his beasts. I remember a bull in his field made what looked like a fearsome approach to a visitor. 'Ach!' said Willie. 'It's jist playin'.'

Whether or not the members of the Life Preservers' Society had stamped over any forgotten rights-of-way I do not know, but I doubt if Mr Parker would have cared very much. He complained that the road was rutted, wet, muddy, uncomfortable and apparently neverending. He called it 'a complete fraud'. He was probably wishing that he had stayed at home, sitting on his doup.

I don't know if Dr Walter Reid was on that outing. He was a veteran member whose eightieth birthday was celebrated by the club at Braemar in 1939. The menu carried a verse which went:

When he is abroad in the hills,
I am told that he frequently yodels,
But he is always glad to get back at night
To his beautiful home at Pitfodels.

As I wrote on another occasion, the whole LPS membership must have echoed that sentiment on the Lumphanan outing.

31

YOKIESHILL

A cut-out figure of a bull stands on top of a farm sign near Longside in Buchan. The sign says 'Yokieshill'. The Scots word 'yokie' means itchy, but how this came to be the name of a farm is a mystery. Nobody really knows the origin of the name, not even the place-name experts. William M. Alexander dodged the issue in his *Place-Names of Aberdeenshire*, giving only the names that were known a few centuries ago – Yokkeishill in 1544 and Yokeshill in 1637.

The 1637 name suggests an alternative to an itchy bull, for it has yoke in it, not yokie. The word 'yoke' has a number of meanings, most of them connected with work, so maybe the sign was intended as a reminder to farm workers that they had to be up and 'yokit', ready for work.

My father, who was brought up on a Buchan farm, often used to say, 'It's time to get yokit.' Time to start work. *Chambers Scots Dictionary* explains 'yokin' (yoking horses, etc) as 'starting a spell of work', and 'yokin time' is said to be a stint or a shift. But there is another curious suggestion – if you are ill-matched in marriage you are ill-yokit.

It is an impressive-sounding word, yokit, a strong, no-nonsense word, a word as Buchan as neep brose and chappit tatties. It appeared more than once in David Toulmin's *Collected Short Stories*. In one of his stories, 'Who would be a gaffer?' he wrote about the gaffers in the old days, who 'walked in at one end of the stable at yoking time and out at the other, snapping out orders as they went. The men said nothing, for woe betide a man gin he back-speired a gaffer in those days.' So, wrote Toulin, 'there wasn't much to be said at yoking time anyway'.

Yokieshill Farm.

Then there was a farmer called Bert Mutch, a 'strushle [rough] brute', who was very unpopular with the men. 'The folk had never quite forgiven the chiel since he kicked his fee-ed loon doon the chaumer stair for sleepin-in; tore him out of bed in his sark tail and kicked him on the bare doup with his tackety boot, nearly breaking the lad's neck in the fall, "By Chove!" he cried, from the top of the stair, "that'll learn ye tae rise in the mornin, and ye'll get no breakfast for yer pains. Get yer breeks on and yoke yer horse or ye'll get mair!" '

Toulmin (or John Reid to give him his real name) knew all about yokin. He would have known fine how Yokieshill got its name for there were farm names scattered like chaff all through his books, although they were fictitious names, conjured up for his story-telling. Kinsourie, Slabsteen, Clayfoons, Fernieden, Kelpieside, Tullymarle, Kingowrie, Shinbrae – on and on it went, names that would have set the onomastic experts jumping up and down with excitement if they had been real.

There were fanciful names in Toulmin's tales, and there were also some odd characters to go along with them, like the Dookit (from the Dookit Farm), a queer mannie, they said, and 'affa religious', and Auld Snorlie from Swineden, who had to tether 'a coo or two' at the roadside because there was no grass in his parks, nothing but stones and thistles, and Auld

Knowie from Knowehead, who lived by the clock and had a gold watch with a lid on its face fastened to his waistcoat by a thin chain.

I've often wondered if some of his characters were based on real-life people. At any rate, the greatest character in Buchan was at Yokieshill itself, and he *was* a real-life individual. Tocher of Yokieshill was said to be the doyen of all the Buchan worthies. He had enormous strength and his graip (fork) had five prongs and was specially made at the smiddy. Nobody could handle it but Tocher and when he left Yokieshill it was taken back to the blacksmith and turned into a grubber, an iron harrow, that had to be pulled by a team of three horses.

Tocher was second horseman and the first morning he was at Yokieshill the grieve told him and the foreman to put their ploughs on carts and take them to the smiddy for remoulding. The foreman was struggling with his plough and Tocher offered to help, but he was told that everyone loaded his own plough at Yokieshill. Tocher went back to his horse, lifted the plough over his head, and threw it into the cart. It went right through the bottom and stuck in the axle.

When Yokies, the farmer, went on holiday he gave Tocher a list of jobs to keep him busy. 'And what div I dee efter that?' asked Tocher. 'Och,' said Yokies, jokingly, 'ye can tak' the slates aff the barn!' When he returned from his holiday he was amazed to see Tocher on the roof of the barn throwing off the slates. 'Have ye deen a' yer wark?' he asked. 'Oh aye,' said Tocher, 'I've jist the barn tae finish!'

This part of Buchan is a store-house of fascinating place names. David Toulim may have got his inspiration from some of them. He wrote about a farm called Clayfoons and there is a Claypots Croft a couple of miles south of Yokieshill. His Bogside marched alongside true-life Buchan names like Bogieneuk, Bogiesavoch and Boglash, and his Blackstob farm lined up with Blackpots at Old Deer and Blacksbog at Longside. There was a Barnyards in his book, 'a muckle sair toon tae work on,' and it wouldn't have been on its own, for there were farmyards in Old Deer, St Fergus, Daviot, Peterhead and Pitsligo. The name was said to be a relic from the large scale farming common until the end of the seventeenth century.

I remember John Reid telling me about one farm that was known to thousands of people. This was Bridge-end at Aikey Brae. Old Briggie, the farmer, had a field there which he said was the best paying field he ever had. He said he never planted anything in it but bicycles. It was the field where folk going to Aikey Fair parked their bikes. It cost you a tanner (sixpence) to park your bike on Briggie's land and there were 'acres of bicyles' dumped in his field on the day of the fair.

But back to Yokies. There was an old ballad that said, 'I took a turn at Yokieshill, the teuchest place I e'er gaed till.' The man who farms the teuchest (toughest) place in Buchan today is Charles Gall, who has been at Yokieshill since 1956, but he couldn't offer any explanation of the name. What he did tell me was that at one time it was called Tickly Mountain. Being tickly – itchy – might have been acceptable, but turning Yokies*hill* into a mountain seemed to be stretching the imagination a bit. Later, I discovered that Yokieshill had appeared in a 1544 list of lands belonging to the Abbey of Deer. It was known then as the Hill of the Small Howe. So much for the mountain theory.

The 1696 Census gave the name as Yockshill. There were seventeen people on the Poll list and it was set out as a ferm toon, with two tenants. Alexander Daniel was one tenant, and he had a wife Jean. He employed a byrewoman, a herd and a weaver. The second tenant was Christian May, who had three sons working on the farm. Both had grassmen or grasswomen, workers who had a cottar house but no land. Daniel employed a 'litle man' and Christian May had a 'litle woman'. *Chambers Scots Dictionary* defined a 'litle man' as 'a junior or adolescent male farm servant' and presumably the same applied to a 'litle woman'.

So that was Yokieshill, past and present, and every time I pass it and see the bull glowering at me from the farm sign I scratch myself and wonder what the name really means.